ALL-TERRAIN
PUSHCHAIR WALKS
Anglesey & Lleyn Peninsula

Zoë Sayer and Rebecca Terry

Published by Sigma Leisure – an imprint of
Sigma Press, 5 Alton Road, Wilmslow, Cheshire SK9 5DY, England.

British Library Cataloguing in Publication Data
A CIP record for this book is available from the British Library.

ISBN: 1-85058-840-6

Typesetting and Design: Sigma Press, Wilmslow, Cheshire.

Cover Photograph: South Stack Lighthouse, Anglesey *(Copyright, Phillip Elsdon)*.

Maps: Zoë Sayer and Rebecca Terry.

Photographs: Zoë Sayer, Keith Jackson, Rebecca Terry and Tracy Whale.

Printed by: Bell and Bain Ltd, Glasgow

Disclaimer: the information in this book is given in good faith and is believed to be correct at the time of publication. No responsibility is accepted by either the author or publisher for errors or omissions, or for any loss or injury howsoever caused. Only you can judge your own fitness, competence and experience. Do not rely solely on sketch maps for navigation; we strongly recommend the use of appropriate Ordnance Survey (or equivalent) maps.

Preface

The rugged coastal scenery of Anglesey and the Lleyn Peninsular are the perfect place to enjoy a walk with your children. There is so much to see while you are there including castles, lighthouses and an abundance of wildlife. The younger your children are when you begin to take them out and about, the more likely they will grow up with a full understanding of the environment around them. The unspoilt beauty of this region of North Wales not only allows you to have fun in the water, animal spotting and picnicking along the way but also teaches both you and the children about some of the local history while you are there.

All-terrain pushchairs are growing in popularity as people begin to realise how versatile they can be. No longer are we restricted to the pavements and side roads of our local towns and countryside. It is now possible to take our children through fields, woods and over mountains in order to show them the full scope of what the country-side has to offer. However, stiles, narrow kissing gates and rocky terrain can still hinder our progress and it is impossible to see such obstacles on a map. We have selected thirty pushchair-friendly walks in Anglesey and the Lleyn peninsular, minimising these obstacles. All routes have been thoroughly tried and tested with babies in pushchairs, so you can now go for a walk with full knowl-edge of the route ahead.

In choosing the walks for this book we have covered a diverse range of terrain in order to show you the best that the area has to offer. The walks range from simple beach strolls to rugged inland hill-top rambles, so there is something for everyone to enjoy. The simple 'at a glance' symbol key and grading system make walk selec-tion easy. You can begin each walk knowing whether there are refreshments and changing facilities available, allowing you to plan ahead. Every walk has background information about the area and an 'in the area' section which suggests other ways to entertain your-selves and the children while you are there.

It has been great fun putting this book together and we hope that you and your children enjoy them as much as we did.

Acknowledgements

Special thanks to Rhodri and Jamie for being the test subjects for this book and to Keef and Phil for accompanying us on many of these walks. Thanks also to Alan Kelly for information Parys Mountain, Adam Voelker for help with research on the area's churches and Lôn Goed, and Jim Ostler for the translation given in Walk 28.

Contents

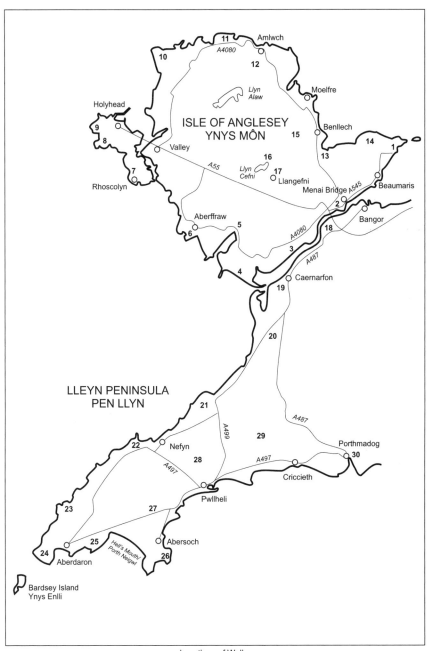

Locations of Walks

Introduction

This book contains thirty walks on Anglesey and the Lleyn Peninsular suitable for an all-terrain pushchair. There are both circular and "there-and-back" routes, and many can be shortened or have worthwhile detours. Walks range from 1 to 4½ miles in length and cover a wide range of difficulty, which we hope will cater for all types of walkers. The walks encompass both coastal and inland areas, so, hopefully, you will find a suitable walk nearby, wherever you are. The walks are not exhaustive and are intended as an introduction to the area. There are many other suitable routes to explore once you know what is possible with a pushchair.

Routes and Grades

We have purposefully made this book as easy to follow as possible. Each walk is accompanied by a simple route map showing the start point and numbers referring to details in the text, as well as obvious features. The maps are intended to be used in conjunction with the relevant Ordnance Survey Explorer map, and the information on them is by no means comprehensive. Details of the relevant map and the starting grid reference are given in the walk summary.

Each walk contains an "at-a-glance" key, which tells you all you need to know to prepare for the walk – distance, difficulty, any stiles, facilities such as toilets or ice cream vans and any hidden costs, so there shouldn't be any nasty surprises when you set off. You can also see whether the walk requires two people to overcome obstacles or if it can be accomplished solo.

The walks have a basic summary detailing points of interest and useful information on the area. We have also included an "in the area" section, suggesting nearby alternative activities for yourself and your family.

You should always allow more time than that recommended. Times given are approximate and based on a speed of two miles an hour. However, not everyone walks at the same speed and the times given do not make allowances for picnics, tantrum breaks or walking toddlers.

It should be noted that circular routes are written in the direction which requires the least effort and are not always reversible! If you are thinking of reversing a walk, read the description carefully to check it is possible.

Fitness

It is assumed that walkers will have a basic level of fitness. Those who consider themselves unfit should only attempt the easiest level of walk and, if necessary, take advice from their doctor. The hardest level of walk should only be attempted by those experienced in both walking and all-terrain pushchair technique.

All-Terrain Pushchairs – Advice for First-Time Buyers

There are now many makes of all-terrain pushchairs (ATPs) on the market. For help in choosing an ATP, here are some of the factors we have come across in researching this and other books:

Ensure your child is old enough for the ATP. Many makes have a reclining position suitable for use from birth, but bear in mind that very young babies should not be bumped around. Seek the manufacturer's advice and choose your walks carefully. Small babies (less than four months) should only be taken on the easiest level of walks and if you are not happy with the terrain, turn round!

Make sure the ATP has pneumatic tyres and good suspension to provide cushioning.

Lightweight prams are better!

Choose a long wheelbase, which makes leverage over obstacles easier than a short wheelbase. The front wheel should be fixed, or, at the very least, lockable. Rear wheels should be quick release.

Check that the pushchair folds easily and that it fits in the boot of your car!

Shop around as it is always worth looking in the shops first and then checking the internet for the same pram at a better price – either new or used.

Single and Double All-Terrain Pushchairs from the 'Mountain Buggy' range. *Reproduced by permission of Chariots All Terrain Pushchairs www.pushchairs.co.uk*

Accessories

A rain cover is essential, especially when out walking in the hills as the weather can change very quickly. Good quality footmuffs are easily available, if not already included in the price; fleece-lining and/or windproofing provides extra comfort.

Sunshades supplement the hood, which generally doesn't extend enough for walking uphill into full sun. Mesh shades are easier to walk with than parasols.

A puncture repair kit and pump are strongly advisable for those emergency situations. You can also fill the tyres with a "goo" designed as an emergency fix for bicycle tyres and which prevents serious deflation.

We've found a pram leash useful, especially on walks with steep drops or steep descents. This is a strap, climbing sling or piece of rope tied to the pram handle and fastened to the wrist. This provides extra security should you accidentally let go of the pushchair, and is more secure than a handbrake.

What to take

For the baby:

✳ Pram with rain cover, sun cover, footmuff and puncture repair kit.

✳ Milk – if you are not breastfeeding, formula milk is easily carried in ready-made cartons or powder sachets. If your baby likes warm milk, carry warm water in a flask to make up hot milk on the move.

✳ Nappies, wipes and nappy bag.

✳ Picnic – sandwiches are easy if your baby eats on his/her own, otherwise take fruit pots, yoghurt or anything easy to open. Don't forget a spoon and take all rubbish home with you.

✳ Snacks to cheer up a bored or peckish baby until you find a picnic spot. We have found that raisins or baby crisps keep them occupied for the longest!

✳ Water/juice

✳ Spare clothes. Layers are best as they can easily be put on or taken off as conditions change. Don't forget that though you may be hot walking uphill, your baby is sat still in the pushchair. Keep checking he/she is not too cold. An all in one fleece is a good buy. Look for one with fold-over ends to keep hands and feet warm – easier than gloves.

✳ Hat, either a sun hat or woolly hat depending on the weather conditions.

✳ Shoes for when your little one wants to get out.

For you

✳ Appropriate shoes (check the guide at the start of the walk) and coat. Keep a light waterproof in the pram ready for emergencies.

✳ Food and drink: it's very easy to forget your own in the rush to pack your baby's feast!

✳ Mobile phone.

✳ Small first aid kit.

✳ This guidebook and the relevant Ordnance Survey map for the walk.

The Countryside Code

✳ Respect – Protect – Enjoy

✳ Do not drop litter. Use a bin or take it home.

✳ Do not stray from public footpaths or bridleways.

✳ Do not pick any plants.

✳ Make no unnecessary noise.

✳ Keep dogs on a lead near livestock and under close control at all other times.

✳ Leave gates as you find them.

✳ Use gates or stiles to cross fences, hedges or walls.

✳ Do not touch livestock, crops or farm machinery.

✳ Keep the natural water supply clean.

✳ Walk in single file and on the right-hand side of roads.

✳ Do not cross railway lines except by bridges.

✳ Guard against the risk of fire.

For information on new access rights, phone 0845 100 3298 or visit www.countrysideaccess.gov.uk.

Why walk?

✳ Walking makes you feel good

✳ Walking reduces stress

✳ Walking helps you see more of your surroundings

✳ Walking helps you return to your pre-pregnancy figure and ......

✳ Walking helps your baby learn about his/her surroundings and nature

Anglesey and the Lleyn Peninsular

These are the perfect locations to inspire you and your children to go walking. The varied terrain provides a range of walks from cliff top rambles to beach strolls.

Anglesey is a large island reached by bridges over the spectacular Menai Straits from the north-west coast of Wales. The scenery is varied and ranges from rugged coastal cliffs and sandy beaches to rolling green countryside inland, with hidden dells and lakes. It is a place steeped in history and legends and much is in evidence of ancient inhabitation, mediaeval castles and more modern industrial endeavours. Holyhead was used by the Romans as a crossing point to Ireland and it is still a busy ferry port. In 1826 Thomas Telford built his famous road from London to Holyhead (now the A5) to connect to the crossing to Dublin which established good communi-cations with the island, especially with the construction of the Menai Bridge, considered by some to be the world's first suspension bridge. Thomas Stevenson of the famous Scottish lighthouse build-ing dynasty constructed the Britannia Bridge to carry the railway onto the island in 1850. In Welsh the island is called Ynys Môn and is often referred to as Mam Cymru (mother of Wales) because it is much more fertile than the more mountainous mainland and in the past supplied most of the grain for the area. This was a dependency recognised by Edward I when England decided to stamp its author-ity on the local population and so the island and the crossing on the Menai Straits became of strategic importance, hence the castle at Beaumaris. As it is an island, many of the walks are coastal or have spectacular sea views, but we have steered away from too many beach walks and you can reach the summits of two of Anglesey's rather modest mountains!

The Lleyn Peninsular protrudes into Cardigan Bay between Porthmadog and Caernarfon in the east to Bardsey Island at the western tip. Between rugged coastal headlands are secluded sandy bays and the interior is dotted with many impressive and imposing hills which are a string of ancient volcanoes. It is a popular area for tourism and can be very busy in the summer months. However, out of season it is very quiet and despite the influx the area remains a heartland of the Welsh language and culture and is home to the

Welsh National Language Centre. In common with Anglesey the area has a wealth of historical sites such as numerous hill forts, mediaeval houses and ancient churches on the pilgrims' route to the abbey on Bardsey Island. It is very easy to achieve a feeling of remoteness and isolation here and to escape everyday life, which increases its attraction to the walker. As with Anglesey, the scenery and terrain is varied, with spectacular coastal scenery and rolling agricultural interior – the area is home to the Lleyn breed of sheep. Pushchair walking potential is limited due to the number of field boundaries crossed by stiles and we have chosen a selection of walks across varied terrains which capture the peaceful ambience of the area.

The walks are along coastal paths, across farmland and through forestry on a combination of public rights of way, forest tracks and access paths. Rights of way on access paths and access land are at the discretion of the landowner and as defined under the Countryside and Rights of Way Act 2000, and though all routes are allowed at time of writing, permission could potentially be withdrawn in the future.

Routes along beaches and some coastal sections are affected by tides. If a walk is tide-dependent we have mentioned this in the introduction and an alternative, there and back route is possible. Always check the tide as on some walks it is possible to be cut off part way across a coastal section. Tide tables are available in most outdoor shops and tourist information centres. Many national newspapers publish tide times and heights (usually on the weather page) or they can be checked on www.britishinformation.com.

Finally, when crossing farmland always pay consideration to livestock. Keep dogs on a lead, older children under control and never disturb any animal you come across. In addition, herds of cows can be problematic and have (fortunately rarely) been known to kill humans by stampeding. On one of the walks, the cows were particularly interested in the pushchair! If you are in any doubt as to your safety, leave the field by the nearest possible exit and abandon the walk.

Further Reading

'All Terrain Pushchair Walks: Snowdonia' makes the perfect companion to this book encompassing 30 walks amongst the mountains and valleys adjoining the area to the east of that covered in this book.

Glossary of Welsh words

Here are the rough translations of some of the words you'll come across on the walks. This is not a comprehensive list, but hopefully some understanding will enhance your enjoyment of the area.

N.B. Welsh words *mutate* – the first letter changes. Some common mutations you might see are shown in brackets.

Aber	River mouth
Aderyn	Bird
Afon	River
Bach, Bychan	Small
Bae	Bay
Bedd	Grave, digging
Betws	Chapel, house of prayer
Brenin	King
Bryn	Hill
Bwlch	Pass
Cadair (Gadair)	Seat
Cae	Field, enclosure
Caer	Fort, citadel
Canol	Centre, middle
Capel	Chapel
Carnedd (Garnedd)	Cairn, rocky hilltop
Carreg	Stone, rock
Castell	Castle
Cefn	Back, ridge
Clogwyn	Cliff
Coch (Goch)	Red
Coed	Wood, forest
Craig	Crag, rock
Crib	Ridge
Croes (Groes)	Cross
Cwm	Valley
Cymru	Wales
Derwen	Oak
Dinas	Fort
Du (Ddu)	Black

Dwr	Water
Dyffryn	Valley
Dynion	Gents
Eglwys	Church
Eryri	Snowdonia
Fferm	Farm
Ffordd	Road
Ffridd	Upland pasture
Ffynnon	Spring, well
Gallt (Allt)	Slope
Glan	Shore, bank
Glas	Blue, green
Gwyn, Wen	White
Gwynt	Wind
Hafod	Summer dwelling
Hen	Old
Hendre	Winter dwelling
Hir	Long
Isaf	Lower
Llwybr Cyhoeddus	Public footpath
Llyn	Lake
Llynau	Lakes
Llys	Court
Lôn	Lane
Maen	Stone
Maes	Field, meadow
Mawr (Fawr)	Big
Merched	Ladies
Melin (Felin)	Mill
Moel (Foel)	Bare hilltop
Môr	Sea
Morfa	Sea-marsh
Mynydd	Mountain
Nant	Brook
Newydd	New
Oer	Cold
Ogof	Cave
Pant	Hollow
Pen	Head
Penrhyn	Peninsula, promontory
Pentref	Village
Plas	Mansion
Pont (Bont)	Bridge
Porth	Port
Preifat	Private

Pwll	Pool
Rhaeadr	Waterfall
Rhyd	Ford
Sarn	Causeway, pavement
Tal	End
Tan	Beneath
Toiledau/Cyfleusterau	Toilets
Traeth	Beach
Tref (Dref)	Town
Twr	Tower
Twysog	Prince
Ty	House
Tyddyn	Farmstead, small-holding
Uchaf	Upper
Ynys	Island
Yr Wyddfa	Snowdon

Some of the unfamiliar letter pronunciations for English speakers are as follows:

dd – *th* as in *the*
f – *v* as in *vole*
ff – *f* as in *ford*
th – *th* as in *thin*
rh – a breathy *r*
ll – put your tongue on your teeth and say "*lllll*" – a very soft "cl"
ch – back of the throat and breathe out, similar to the Scottish ch in loch
s – always soft as in *soft*
u – *i* as in *big*
w – *oo* as in *soon*
y – at the start of a word *u* as in *butter*
y – elsewhere, *i* as in *big*
e – as in *bed*
o – as in *top*
a – as in *dad*

Circular route.

There and back. Route is non-circular.

Easy route with very few hills.

Moderate exertion. Some gentle ascents and descents.

Hard going. Route incorporates some steep inclines.

Easy terrain, trainers suitable.

Muddy and wet. Wellington boots or hiking boots are required.

Rough terrain. Rocky and uneven ground, hiking boots recommended.

Stile

Icecream van on route!

Tea shop.

Pub/Hotel.

Picnic table.

Children's play ground

Trains.

Ducks!

Toilets.

Solo. Walk can be accomplished alone.

At least two people required to complete walk. Pushchair may need to be lifted over obstacles.

Money required for parking, entrance fee or rail fare.

Key to symbols

Walk 1: Penmon Point and Priory

Allow: *1 hour 15 minutes*

This is a wonderful tranquil walk along the coast of the eastern tip of Anglesey, which gives great views over Snowdonia and the northern coast of Wales. At the beginning of the walk you will see the ruins of Penmon Priory. This monastery is reputed to have been founded by St Seiriol, a 6th-century holy man. However, Viking raids destroyed all evidence of the original building and the ruins that you see today are the remains of the priory that was rebuilt in the 12th century. This Augustinian priory was dissolved in 1538 and was taken over by the Bulkeleys of Beaumaris who enclosed much of the land as a deer park and built the dovecote.

Penmon Point (Trwyn Du) is the half way mark of this walk and from here you are rewarded with fantastic views over Trwyn Du lighthouse and Puffin Island. Puffin Island is called Ynys Seiriol (Seriol's Island) in Welsh and it is said that St Seiriol is buried here – the building you can see is reputedly a monk's cell. The island was once home to a large colony of puffins, but their numbers were decimated by rats and only a small number of breeding pairs remain. Since 1998 a program has been underway to exterminate the rats and to encourage the return of these delightful birds.

This walk should only be attempted in the direction written due to the presence of steps. Though there is one stile, this is avoidable following the alternative directions.

Map: Ordnance Survey 1:25000 Explorer OL263 – grid reference 630807

Distance: 2 miles (3 km)

Getting there: From Beaumaris, take the B5109 towards Llangoed. Just before the village of Llangoed, take the right turn to Penmon. Follow this winding road until you reach Penmon Priory. Park in the Priory and Dovecote car park, taking care not to block farm access gates.

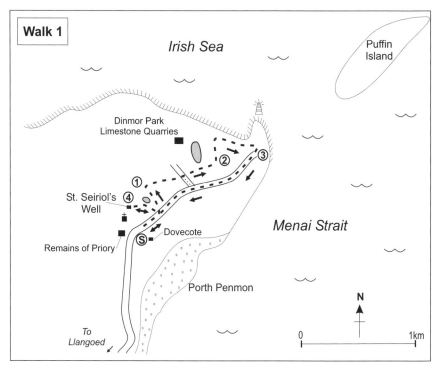

Leave the car park and walk up the toll road straight ahead of you. Pass the dovecote on your right.

> The dovecote was built around 1600 and has a stone pillar in the centre which provides support for the ladder giveing access to the nests. The nests are in small cubby holes, which are built into the walls.

Go round the bend, pass a driveway on your right and you will then see a gateway and ladder stile on your left. Go through the gate and head across the field on the grassy track towards a gateway in a high wall, once the wall of the Deer Park.

Don't go through the gateway. Turn right just before it and follow the wall along the edge of the field until you reach a stile. Go over the stile, turn right and head up the track towards the road. Go through a gap in the hedge to your left, signposted with a yellow arrow and a coastal footpath marker.

If you want to avoid this stile, continue along the road from the car park until you get to the brow of the hill and then turn left down a gated tarmac track. Go through the gap in the hedgerow on your right (opposite a small stile) marked by the yellow arrow and coastal footpath marker and continue along the route described below.

1. Go down a grassy track to a ladder stile which can be avoided by going through a gap in the wall to your left. Keep following the main track.

    The bell that you may be able to hear is that of Trwyn Du lighthouse which stands in the small channel between Penmon Point and Puffin Island. As you come out of the hawthorn bushes you will get great views over the Great Orme and the hills above Conwy and Llanfairfechan

    Go down the steps at the brow of the hill as the lighthouse comes into view. Continue along the path towards the yellow marker arrow and up two small steps at the next brow.

2. Turn left at the top of the small hill and walk out to the headland. You will be able to see the quarries on your left, which supplied much of the building stone in the area. When you get to the coast turn right and follow the grassy track along the edge of the low cliffs to Penmon Point.

    These are unprotected cliff edges so be sure to keep children away from the edge.

3. Once you reach Penmon Point walk back to the car park along the road.

    There are a café and toilets at Penmon Point as well as a pebbly beach for the kids to play on.

4. Just before you get to the car park, turn right to view the monastic fish pond (with friendly ducks!) and follow the path to St Seriol's well. Return to the car park.

Penmon Lighthouse and Puffin Island

St Seriol's well is a resurgence at the base of a small limestone cliff. The water coming from the spring was said to have healing properties and a small building was constructed around it, dating from 1710, though the low seats around the well may be earlier.

In the area

Menai Straits Cruises (www.starida.co.uk) offer boat trips around Puffin Island and past the islands and bridges of the Menai Straits. Both trips offer views of spectacular scenery. Trips depart from and can be booked in Beaumaris.

Museum of Childhood Memories, Beaumaris, is interesting to adults and children alike and shows how family interests have changed over the past 150 years. Exhibits include teddy bears, dolls houses and arcade machines. Traditional toy shop next door. Easter – September, 10.30am-5.30pm. 01248 712498.

Walk 2: Telford's Suspension Bridge and Ynys Tisilio, Menai Bridge

Allow: 1 hour

This walk takes you along the southern banks of the Menai Straits, through the nature reserve of Coed Cyrnol and to Ynys Tisilio, a small island reached by a narrow causeway. On the island is the church of St Tisilio, which is believed to have been established by the 6th-century Welsh saint, after whom it is named. The present building dates back to the 1400s but its origins are unknown. The route then takes you back over the causeway and along the Belgian Promenade. This promenade was built by first world war refugees between 1914-1916 and gives great views over the straits and the suspension bridge.

Telford's Suspension Bridge was the largest bridge of its kind at that time and was the first crossing over the Menai Straits. It was designed to have 100ft of clear space below in order to allow the passage of tall sailing ships. Stone for the arches was mined in the local Penmon quarries (see walk 1) and carried down the Straits by boat. The bridge was finally opened in 1826 and reduced the journey from London to Holyhead from 36 hours to 27.

Map: Ordnance Survey 1:25000 Explorer OL263 – grid reference 554719

Distance: 1¼ miles (2 km)

Getting there: Park in the car park near the Co-op, signposted to Coed Cyrnol. The car park is located in between two roundabouts on the A5 just north of the Menai Suspension Bridge. There are picnic tables and an information board in the car park.

To avoid the steps at beginning of the walk, go back under the car park entrance barrier, turn right and then immediately right again

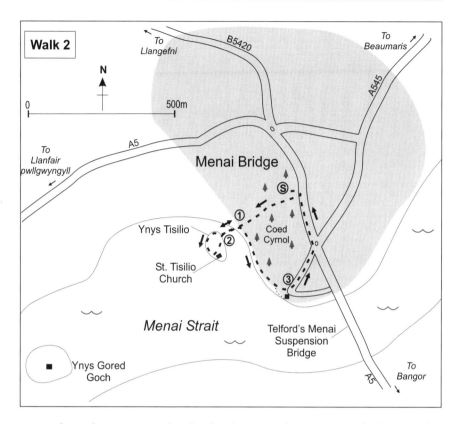

onto a broad tarmac track which takes you down through the woods. This is signposted with a disabled marker.

Coed Cyrnol is a broad-leaved woodland consisting predominantly of beech trees and is especially beautiful during the autumnal leaf fall. The woodland floor is carpeted with bluebells in spring.

1. Follow this track all the way down to the foreshore ignoring the path up to the left. Once on the foreshore, go across the causeway to Ynys Tisilio, which has a small historic church on it.

   Go through the gate into the church yard and turn right to walk around the church grounds.

   There are lots of ducks and sea birds on the shore and lovely views through the woodland. As you go round the corner Stephenson's

St Tisilio's Church

Britannia Bridge, built in 1850, comes into view. This bridge, originally only a railway bridge, now takes the road and railway from the Welsh mainland onto Anglesey. In front of the bridge you will see the island Ynys Gored Goch with an isolated house which has its own fish farm.

Pass the yew trees in the graveyard and follow the path round to the Church of St. Tisilio, which dates back to 630 AD. Turn left at the church and walk down the path back towards the causeway.

2. Go through the yew arch and gates, back across the causeway and then turn right to continue along the foreshore. You are now walking along the Belgian Promenade, which has numerous benches along its length. As you continue along the promenade, Telford's Menai Suspension Bridge comes into view.

A gateway on the right leads into a seating area and to a stone and shingle beach, once a very popular bathing area with many beach huts.

If you go on to the beach, be warned that the currents in the Straits are treacherous. Keep children under control near the water.

3. Turn left past the beach and head up the hill back towards the road. Turn left again onto the road and continue up the hill taking care for cars. When you reach the main road turn left past the Anglesey Arms Hotel. Continue along the main road until you reach the car park. On your right you will pass a building which hosts a bridges exhibition.

In the area

Beaumaris Castle is a stunning example of technical perfection! This moated castle was the last of Edward's Welsh fortresses to be built. Concentric defences with arrow-slits, portcullises and murder holes provide a great setting for little imaginations to run wild. Open all year. 01248 810361.

Pili Palas is a zoo of minibeasts where you will be surrounded by butterflies amongst lush vegetation and waterfalls. Café, shop and soft play area. (www.pilipalas.co.uk)

Walk 3: Llanidan and the Menai Straits, Brynsiencyn

Allow: *2 hours*

Llanidan is a tiny village on the shore of the Menai Straits near Brynsiencyn. This walk takes you along country lanes and farm tracks around some beautiful countryside with open views up and down the Straits and across to Snowdonia.

Though this is a fairly flat walk, it has a difficult grading because of a long, tough stretch across a pebbly beach. For this reason we also recommend two people (to take it in turns!) but there are no lifts and so it could be accomplished solo.

Check the tide before you set off as the beach is under water at the highest tides. If you find this is the case, it is still a nice, easy walk down the lane to the shore and back.

Map: Ordnance Survey 1:25000 Explorer OL263 – grid reference 484670

Distance: 4 miles (6.5 km)

Getting there: Follow the A4080 from Llanfairpwllgwyngyll to Brynsiencyn. Park in the car park on the left as you come into the village. Toilets (closed in winter) and information boards.

Walk out of the car park past the toilets and down the lane, where you get good views across Snowdonia.

As you pass Llanidan Farm on the left, with its lovely old barns, you get your first view of the Menai Straits through the trees.

Continue straight ahead ignoring a footpath sign on your right and a driveway on your left.

Straight ahead is Plas Llanidan, dating back to 1631, but which has been subsequently extended. This was the home of the "Copper

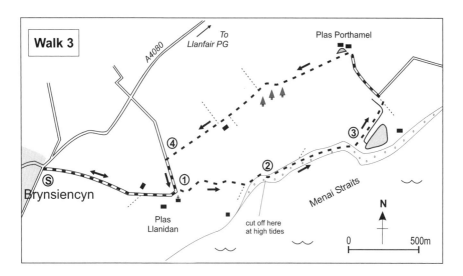

King" Thomas Williams whose fortune came from Anglesey's copper
mines, including Parys Mountain (Walk 12). Look out for peacocks in
the orchard. Just past the house you can see Llanidan old church,
dating back to the 14th century, but now privately owned.

1. At the junction, bear right following the wall on your right. Once
   past the church, follow the track, now rougher, round to the left
   and downhill.

   As you get to the straits, you come to a junction. Ignore the driveway to the right and follow the little yellow arrow to the left
   Continue on to the shore of the Straits.

   If you don't fancy the rough push across the beach, or the tide is in,
   then this is the point to turn around. Have a look at the lovely views
   up and down the Straits and play on the pebbly beach before you
   turn back.

2. Turn onto the pebbly beach and push along wherever you find
   easiest. This is a tough push and lasts for about 750m. Continue
   past the first driveway as your ordeal by pebbles is not over yet!
   Carry on towards the white house on the next headland.

Wildlife pool on the shores of the Menai Straits

Look out for seabirds as you push along the shore, including herons and oystercatchers.

Continue around the bay until you reach a gate and a ladder stile. Carefully open the rickety gate next to the stile and push through into the field.

On your right is a pool, where you may see flocks of birds.

3. Head up the grassy track between the wall and the stream until you reach a ford. Push through the ford and head to a gate. Go through the gate and turn left onto a track and left again onto a metalled lane.

Continue up the lane until you come to a large house, Plas Porthamel, dating back to 1653. Follow the lane as it bends round to the left in front of the house and its pond. Continue down the muddy track, not the grassy path towards a stile.

Follow the track past a small wood, ignoring a footpath sign to your right. Carry straight on past a white house, ignoring private driveways to your left. The track is now tarmac again, and you continue until you reach a T-junction.

4. At the junction turn left, looking out for cars and farm vehicles. This brings you back to Llanidan, where you turn right to walk back up the lane you came down at the start of the walk. Continue up the lane until you reach the car park.

In the area

Hooton's Homegrown, near Brynsiencyn, is a farm shop and pick-your-own. There is various fruit to pick and the shop sells the farm's vegetables, meat, cakes and preserves. There is a café serving local produce. Toilets with changing facilities. Open all year, 10am-5.30pm. (01248 430322.)

Plas Newydd, Llanfairpwllgwyngyll, the home of the Marquess of Anglesey, sits on the shores of the Menai Straits and has a famous mural by the artist Rex Whistler in the dining room. There are walks in the extensive gardens, boat trips along the Straits and excellent woodland obstacle course for kids. Café and toilets. March – November 12pm-5pm (www.nationaltrust.org.uk/wales).

Walk 4: Newborough Warren and Ynys Llanddwyn

Allow: *2 hours*

This walk takes you through forest and along beaches to the beautiful island of Llanddwyn and there are plenty of great picnic spots along the way. There are fantastic sea views throughout and also views over Snowdonia and the Lleyn Peninsular. This nature reserve has one of the finest and largest dune systems in Britain. Newborough Warren was formed in the 13th century when violent storms buried farming land under a blanket of sand. To prevent further loss of land Queen Elizabeth I passed a law protecting marram grass. This grass stabilised the dunes and the warren is now home to a number of specialist plants and invertebrates.

Llanddwyn Island was named after St Dwynwen, the Welsh patron saint of lovers. Legend says that Dwynwen fell in love with Maelon but rejected his advances because her father wished her to marry another. She wished to be released from the unhappy love and dreamed that she was given a potion to do this but the potion turned Maelon to ice. She then prayed that she be granted three wishes: that Maelon be revived, all true lovers find happiness and that she should never again wish to be married. She retreated to Llanddwyn Island where she led the life of a hermit.

Check the tide times before you set off for this walk because the island can become cut off during very high tides. Those with dogs should be aware that they are not allowed on the beach between 1st May and 30th September.

Map: Ordnance Survey 1:25000 Explorer OL263 – grid reference 405634

Distance: 4 miles (6.5 km)

Getting there: From the village of Newborough on the A4080 take the turning opposite the shop towards Llys Rhosyr and the beach.

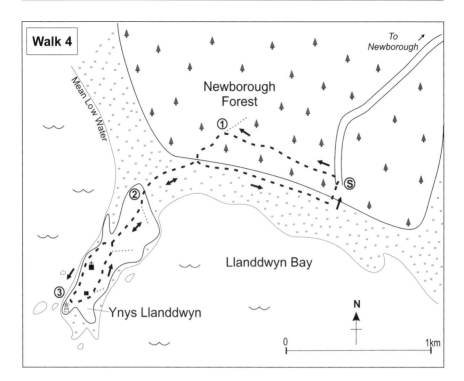

Go through the pay barrier at the end of the road (you'll need change!) and continue right to the end where you will find a car park. There are toilets, picnic tables and an information board here.

Walk back up to the small roundabout from the car park and go straight across onto a forestry track, which is tarmac to begin with, and past a yellow and black barrier. The path is marked with red and blue way markers.

Just before the end of the tarmac section of this path there is a picnic area up to the right with an information board telling you all about the sand dunes.

Stay on the broad gravel track, which takes you through the tall pines of Newborough Forest (red markers), ignoring paths off to the right.

As you reach the brow of the hill you will get your first views over

the sea and Llanddwyn Island. There are also great views of
Snowdonia from the beach.

1. Turn left at the t-junction and keep going to the end of the track.
    Go down the small path to the left just before the end of the track,
    which takes you onto the beach.

    Turn right onto the beach following the curve to Llanddwyn
    Island. When you pass the rocks, head straight across the beach
    to the information board and follow the broad track to the right of
    this (don't turn left up the steps).

    The rocks here are Precambrian pillow lavas, which are the remains
    of submarine volcanic eruptions. They have a characteristic rounded
    shape, formed as the lava oozed out of fissures on the sea floor
    and cooled rapidly on contact with cold sea water. If you look
    carefully, you can clearly see the outlines of the individual pillows.

2. Walk up the track through rocks and sand dunes. Go over the
    cattle grid and turn immediately right up the white shell path.

    You will be able to see the old lighthouse ahead of you, a cross and
    ruins of Llanddwyn church which was used for bombing target
    practice! There are great views of the rocks and sea down to the
    right but be careful if you have toddlers as there is no protection
    on the cliffs. There are a few shallow steps on the path, which can
    be avoided with care.

    Keep following the path along the edge of the island past the
    church and downhill to the right of the cross.

    The large cross is dedicated to Queen Victoria's 60th jubilee and is
    made of Penmon limestone from the quarries of Walk 1. Past the
    lighthouse you will be able to see the Lleyn Peninsular and Bardsey
    Island.

3. Turn left along a white shell path just before you reach the light-
    house steps. At the fork in the path turn left, head slightly uphill
    and follow the path round the headland to the Pilots' Cottages.

Celtic cross, Llanddwyn Island

There are some canons here. Pass in front of the cottages and continue along the path heading back along the island towards the church.

The Pilots' cottages were built to house the pilots who guided ships into the Menai Straits. The cottages now contain an exhibition about the island but it is only open during the holiday season.

Pass the church and the Celtic cross and continue along the path and over the cattle grid to the end of the island.

Turn right onto the beach, pass the pillow lavas and continue along the beach until you see the car park entrance on the left (marked with a post and a life buoy). If you don't want to walk along the beach simply retrace you steps along the forest track.

In the area

The **Isle of Anglesey Riding Centre**, Dwyran, offers rides along the shores of the Menai Straits with horses and ponies to suit all ages and abilities. Children can take short lead-rein rides and learn about horse care. Riding hats provided (www.tal-y-foel.co.uk).

Tacla Taid, near Newborough, is Anglesey's transport museum featuring cars, motorcycles, tractors, army vehicles and even earth moving machines. Café featuring local produce and a children's play area. Open Easter to October, 10.30am- 5.30pm (01248 440344).

Walk 5: Malltraeth Cob and Nature Pool

Allow: *1 hour 30 minutes*

This is a lovely easy walk with plenty to see along the way. The walk begins from Malltraeth, which is one of the most famous bird watching spots in Wales. The extensive mud and sand of the estuary along with the saltmarshes and lagoons provide the perfect habitat for a rich variety of bird life. The walk passes along the mile-long cob embankment. This is a great spot for bird watching as there are seabirds to one side and many ducks and other wildfowl to the other on Malltraeth Pool. It is also possible to see peregrine falcon, buzzards and sparrowhawks from here.

The turning point for the walk is Llyn Parc Mawr, a man-made wildlife pool within Newborough Forest. This is a breeding spot for Curlew, lapwing and ducks in the summer. Large starling roosts can be seen in autumn and a number of wildfowl make it their home during the winter months.

Map: Ordnance Survey 1:25000 Explorer OL263 – grid reference 407687

Distance: 3¾ miles (6 km)

Getting there: Park in the village of Malltraeth which is on the A4080 between Newborough and Aberffraw. There are also two car parks at the southern end of the cob near the nature pool if you want to do a shorter walk.

Leave the car park and follow the footpath sign (blue bird) over the bridge and towards the cob. Once over the bridge the footpath then passes through a kissing gate, through the palisade fencing and onto the cob. Follow this easy gravel path all the way along the cob towards the forest, passing Malltraeth Pool to your left.

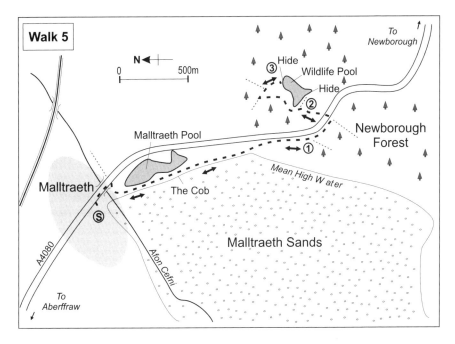

There are great views of the railway viaduct behind you and the estuary and sea to your right. There are benches all the way along the cob so plenty of opportunity to stop and admire the views.

1. Go through the barrier and into the car park at the southern end of the cob. Go straight ahead, past the entrance to the car park and to a notice board where there are footpath signs and three steps. Follow the footpath sign along the small path, which runs parallel to the road.

   Keep going until you get to a track where you turn left and carefully cross the main road. Once over the road follow the path straight ahead to Llyn Parc Mawr which is signposted with a brown sign to the Wildlife Pool. Go left at the fork in the track, not right past a barrier. Continue past a further car park and picnic tables.

2. Once past the picnic tables, turn left and head down the path towards the bird hides. Continue along the woodland path

Railway viaduct, Malltraeth

following the white marker posts in the direction of Birch Hide. Turn right at the next junction onto a broad forest track, and then when the track bends to the left, fork right to continue straight ahead.

3. The wildlife pool can only be seen from the hide so park the push-chair at the bottom of the hide steps and carry the baby up.

On a quiet day the hide is a lovely warm and tranquil spot for some lunch!

Return to the track from the hide and return to your car along the same route.

In the area

Foel Farm Park, Newborough, is a real working farm where you can meet and feed the animals, take a tour by tractor or quad bike and ride on the ponies. For mum and dad there is the Chocolate Farm where you can indulge in hand-made chocolates or have a family meal in the café. Open March – October, 10.30am – 5.30pm (www.foelfarmpark.co.uk).

Anglesey's **Model Village**, Newborough, is set in 1 acre of land-scaped gardens. The models are 1/12 size and include famous Anglesey landmarks. There is a model garden railway and kids can ride an engine round the picnic and play area. Tea rooms and Anglesey ice cream. March – September from 10.30am (01248 440477).

Walk 6: Aberffraw Estuary

Allow: *1 hour 30 minutes*

Aberffraw, on Anglesey's southern coast, was the Mediaeval court of the Kings and Princes of Wales, and was most important under the reign of Llywelyn ap Iorwerth (Llywelyn the Great). The village is situated on an estuary amongst beautiful coastal scenery, with rocky headlands, expansive sand-dunes and secluded beaches.

This walk takes you along the edge of the estuary and around the headland, before returning on farm tracks and country lanes to the village. There are a couple of secluded bays along the route with sandy beaches, which are perfect to break the walk for a picnic and a play!

Map: Ordnance Survey 1:25000 Explorer OL262 – grid reference 357689

Distance: 2½ miles (3.75 km)

Getting there: Head along the A4080 to the village of Aberffraw. Park in the car park by the old bridge. Toilets are located over the bridge in the village.

From the car park, walk over the bridge and turn left to follow the road down the estuary.

> Aberffraw Old Bridge was built in 1731 and is a classic example of a single span bridge. Bridges of this style proliferated in Wales with the increase in use of the horse and cart.

Continue along the sea shore until the road turns down a slip into the water. At this point, follow the coastal footpath sign to the right up a muddy path between two walls. When the path opens out, turn immediately left past a metal gate, following the arrows along a narrow path between the houses. This brings you back down to the estuary shore.

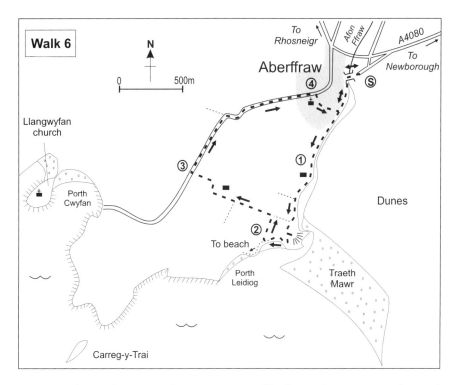

Drop down four wooden steps to walk along the water's edge. (If the tide is in, you can walk along the raised embankment, but this gets very narrow before dropping down 5 awkward stone steps to rejoin the shore path.)

To your left, you can see the vast expanse of the sand dunes. This is one of the largest expanses of coastal sand dunes in Wales. The dunes have been stabilised by natural vegetation, including marram grass and lyme grass, and blue sea holly can be seen at their southern end.

1. Walk along the sea shore and go round to the left of a white house. This stretch is slightly rocky, with two steps downwards. Continue along the shore, which is wet in places, even at low tide.

    Continue until you meet a track. Cross this track and head for the kissing gate straight ahead. Lift the pushchair over the gate and

Aberffraw estuary

head up the sandy, rocky path between gorse and bracken. At the fork in the paths, follow the double arrow to the left.

To get to the viewpoint, push up the hill to your left where you can sit on the bench to take in the view across the bay to the large beach, Traeth Mawr, the Lleyn Peninsula and Snowdonia. Return back down the hill and turn left to continue along the beach edge.

The cairn at this viewpoint is the only evidence of Middle Stone Age man in Gwynedd. It is the remains of a camp and dates back 9000 years!

2. At the next arrows, double back to your right, away from the direction indicated.

To get to a lovely beach, follow the arrows to the left, along the shore and down some easy steps – a great place for a picnic!

Follow the grassy path along and round to the left towards a kissing gate (look out for livestock as there may be cows in this area). Lift over the gate and head straight up the track in front of you.

Ignore the first junction to your right and at the second junction, continue straight ahead. Keep following the track as it bends round to the right.

At the top of the hill, is a lovely view across the southern coast of Anglesey to Snowdonia. To your left, you can see a small church sat isolated on an island in the bay. This is the old church of Llangwyfan, which was in existence in 1254 and added to in the 14th and 15th centuries. Parts of the church, bigger than it is today, were demolished in the 19th century and the sea had eroded the site of the church, with many of the graves falling into the water. Today, the church is again in danger of erosion by the sea.

3. Follow the track until it reaches a road and turn right to follow the road for about 1km back to the village, watching out for traffic.

4. When you get to the village church, turn right down Bro Branwen to follow a small path to the right of the hall. Join a road and head downhill until you reach the estuary once more. Turn left, then right over the bridge and back to your car.

In the area

Anglesey Sea Zoo is a fascinating aquarium housing Anglesey's many resident sea creatures and some interesting foreign visitors such as sea horses and corals. Visit the lobster hatchery, see how the famous Halen Mon Anglesey Salt is extracted or play a round of Capt Jake's Crazy Golf. Café and toy shop. Open February – October, check for times (www.angelseyseazoo.co.uk).

Llanfairpwllgwyngyllgogerychwyrndrobwllllantysiliogogogoch Station – visit the station with the world's longest name! You can also visit the Siding's Restaurant for refreshments in the neighbouring outlet centre.

Walk 7: Rhoscolyn, Holy Island

Allow: 1 hour 15 minutes

This is a beautiful coastal walk that begins in the sheltered cove of Borth Wen. This award winning beach is a great place for the kids to play either before or after you have completed the walk. The route initially follows the Anglesey coastal path and rewards you with fantastic views of the southern coast of Holy Island. The walk then returns via St Gwenfaen's church and follows the road down past the White Eagle Inn. This pub is an excellent baby friendly place to stop for refreshments on the way back to the car.

There is the option of extending this walk further along the coastal path. However, this does involve lifting the pushchair over a number of narrow kissing gates and so is not for the faint-hearted.

Map: Ordnance Survey 1:25000 Explorer 262 – grid reference 272751

Distance: 2 miles (3 km)

Getting there: Park in the Rhoscolyn beach car park. There are toilets here but they are locked out of season.

Walk down the small path, along the board walk and onto the beach. Turn right and walk along the beach with the sea to your left.

The small island you will see ahead is Ynys Defaid (Sheep Island).

As you walk along the beach turn right up to the wall, go up the nine steps and follow the footpath along and back down onto the beach. If the tide is out it is possible to miss out this section of footpath and stay on the beach.

1. Go up the ramp which takes you off the beach onto an uneven track which is signposted as private land, footpath only. Continue along as this becomes a gravel track passing the old life-boat house on your left.

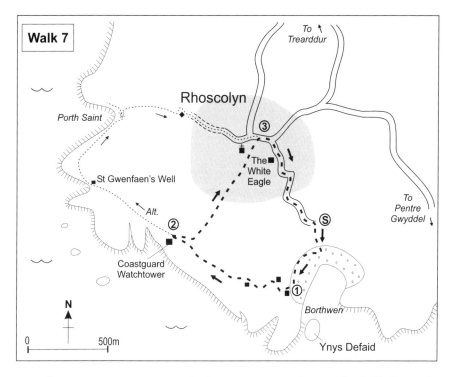

When you pass Boatman's Cottage turn right up the hill through some gateposts marked as Bryn Eithin. Before you reach the house follow the footpath arrows to the right through a gap in the wall and across an area of grass. The footpath then turns back to the left, becomes a narrow dirt path and continues along between some walls. Eventually you will come to a narrow kissing gate, which you will have to lift the pushchair over and then walk straight across the field.

There are fantastic views across the Irish Sea to your left. Within the field you should be able to see the marks of an ancient furrow system on your left.

Lift the pushchair over the second kissing gate and continue following the path up the hill straight ahead. Eventually you will come to the coastguard's watchtower.

Alongside the coastguard's watchtower is a memorial to Dennis

Walk 7: Rhoscolyn, Holy Island

They'll only pose with ATPs!

Stephenson Wood (1934-2001) a geologist who studied the Precambrian rock of Rhoscolyn.

2. Turn right here and follow the grass and gravel track away from the coast, around the corner to a gate.

It is possible to follow the coastal path straight ahead which takes you past St Gwenfaen's well, round the headland to the bay of Porth Saint. From here you can turn right after a small bridge and head back inland towards Rhoscolyn (see alternative route on map). This route gives fantastic views but does involve six more lifts over narrow kissing gates, although three of these can sometimes be avoided if gates are unlocked.

Lift the pushchair over the gate, continue through a second gate and carry on along the track past houses on your left. Continue past an old gothic school building on your right and the church on your left. Go through the gate onto the road, looking out for traffic.

3. Turn right onto the road and right again, following the signs to Traeth/Beach. Walk along the road, past the White Eagle Inn, back to the car park and the beach!

In the area

Silver Bay is a beautiful, long, sandy beach near Rhoscolyn. It is backed by dunes and is ideal for swimming and building sandcastles.

Ellin's Tower Seabird Centre at South Stack has spectacular views across the cliffs and the Irish Sea. Friendly staff can help you spot the nesting sea birds, peregrines and choughs. Easter – September 10am-5.30pm (www.rspb.org.uk/cymru).

Walk 8: Penrhyn Mawr, Trearddur

Allow: 1 hour 30 minutes

This is a nice easy walk that gives you great views of rocky headlands and deep-cut inlets known as zawns. There are great views over the bay of Abraham's Bosom and up to South Stack lighthouse and Holyhead Mountain. You will also be able to see down the coast to Trearddur Bay and over the sea to the Lleyn Peninsular on a clear day. If you can make it here for early evening then you will find that it is the perfect place from which to watch the sunset.

The walk follows gentle grassy paths along this remote headland. Though the cliffs are lower than at South Stack, keep children under control as the drops are unprotected. However, there are plenty of grassy areas for picnics and games!

Map: Ordnance Survey 1:25000 Explorer OL262 – grid reference 216803

Distance: 3 miles (4 km)

Getting there: Park in the car park down a side-road between Trearddur and South Stack (as grid reference).

Walk down the signposted footpath past a metal bollard marked "Keep Clear".

You are heading out towards the coast and will be able to see South Stack lighthouse and Holyhead Mountain on your right. The end of the Lleyn Peninsular will soon come into view on your left.

Bear left at the fork in the path and then, when the path forks again, bear right following the yellow arrow. Continue to the coast and head left along the coastline around the headland, ignoring any small paths off to either side.

The coastal cliffs here are cut by zawns, deep gulleys eroded by the sea where the rock is softer. Keep children away from the cliff edges, but there is plenty of grass for them to run around on!

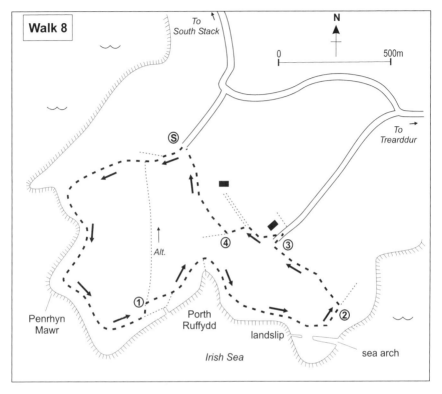

1. Turn left up a broad path just before you reach the wooden fences around a deep zawn.

   If you want a short-cut back to the car park, follow this track up to a wooden post, turn right and continue to the car park.

   Turn right at the next junction onto a broad track and follow it along. You come to steps down to a pebbly beach in Porth Ruffydd, pass the steps and turn right to head round the next headland.

   Out to sea you can see the Lleyn Peninsula and the pointed hills of the Rivals (walk 21). At the end of the peninsula is Bardsey Island, a place of pilgrimage. Straight ahead you have views along the undulating coastline of Holy Island, towards the Anglesey mainland. The cliffs here are host to flocks of seabirds.

Continue to an arrow-post and turn right again heading downhill. Cross a small stream and head back uphill. Continue along the coast. As the ground gets more gravely, keep away from the cliff edge as the land here is slowly slipping into the sea.

Once past the landslip, continue along the grassy path which starts to bear around to the left. Go past the "island" to your right and keep heading towards a gate.

South Stack lighthouse from Penrhyn Mawr

This island is actually just attached to the headland by a sea arch.

2. Just before you reach the kissing gate, turn left to head straight up a gravely path. Continue to a metal barrier and pass it to the right onto a metalled lane.

3. At the next junction, turn left to head towards a white house. Continue down the track as it curves past the very neat garden, and 50 yards on turn left down a path through two metal posts.

4. At the next junction, turn right through the gorse (straight ahead is far too wet!) down a grassy path which can be quite boggy in places. Follow this path back to the car park, ignoring any turns to the left and right.

In the area

Trearddur Bay Beach is ideal for families as it has a protected swimming area, clearly marked by buoys. There is a sandy beach and rockpools and beach wardens are on duty in summer. The toilets have changing facilities and there are cafés and shops in the village. No dogs on certain areas – check car parks for details.

Tyn-Morfa Riding Centre, Rhosneigr, specialises in beach rides. Children over 6 and beginners are welcome. Rides last for about 1 hour and hats are included in the cost. (www.tynmorfa.com).

Walk 9: South Stack, Holyhead

Allow: 1 hour 30 minutes

The area around South Stack (Ynys Lawd) and Holyhead Mountain, on Holy Island, Anglesey, is a spectacular landscape of plunging cliffs, rocky headlands and expansive sea. It is popular with bird-watchers due to the abundance of nesting sea birds, and the sheer cliffs provide some of the best climbing in North Wales.

The walk takes you around the headland above South Stack and its lighthouse, along the cliff tops overlooking Gogarth Bay and back along tracks to a settlement of Iron Age huts. The scenery is stunning, and on a clear day the views stretch across to the Wicklow Mountains in Ireland. The paths are good but exposed and there is no protection along the cliffs.

Due to unprotected cliffs along this walk, we strongly recommend the use of a pushchair leash.

Map: Ordnance Survey 1:25000 Explorer OL262 – grid reference 210819

Distance: 2½ miles (3 km)

Getting there: From Holyhead or Trearddur, follow the brown tourist signs to South Stack. Turn up the road towards South Stack and park in the RSPB car park on the left.

From the car park, take the disabled access gravel footpath, past the emergency access sign, to Ellin's Tower. There are unprotected high cliffs not far from this path so keep all children under control.

> To your left is the Irish Sea, and on a clear day you can see the Wicklow Mountains

Keep heading along the path towards a white castellated outline of Ellin's Tower. There are benches along the path to admire the view!

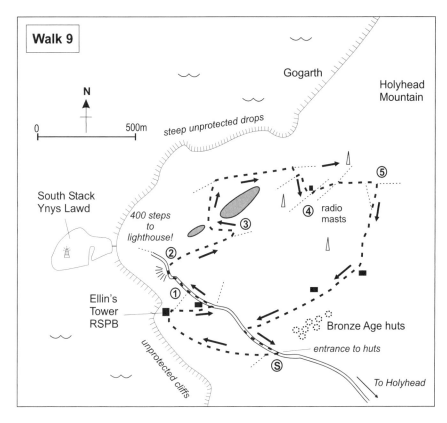

Ellin's Tower is an RSPB bird centre, where you can view breeding sea birds, including puffins. It is open from Easter to September 10.00am – 5.30pm.

1. From Ellin's Tower, go up nine steps and continue along the path until you reach a bench with a good view of South Stack lighthouse.

The lighthouse was designed by Daniel Alexander and built in 1809. Nowadays, it is automated and is open to the public during the main holiday season when you can take a trip to the top of the tower. It is not pushchair friendly, as there are over 400 steps to access the base of the lighthouse – and that's before you've even gone up the tower!

South Stack and lighthouse

Just after the bench, turn right to avoid a flight of steps, and head diagonally up the hillside towards a white building. Head up 12 easy steps to reach the café car park.

To avoid all the steps, the café can be accessed by walking up the road from where you left your car.

At the café, turn left to walk along the road and up the hill.

2. Take the first turning on the right up a metalled track marked by a weathered footpath sign. Head past a metal barrier and up the hill.

Just before a rocky knoll on your left, take a left-hand fork off the metalled track to head down a rough gravel path towards a lake. Before you reach the lake, turn left again to zigzag back in the direction you came from. Walk between the two lakes along a bumpy and rocky path.

3. At the T-junction, turn right along a well defined gravel path along the cliff-top. Make sure you are using a pushchair leash at this point and that your baby is securely fastened in.

As you reach the end of the lake, in the distance you can see the small islands of The Skerries, with their red and white striped lighthouse. This was the most expensive lighthouse ever bought by Trinity House, the company that manages the lighthouses of England and Wales. The light was built by William Trench, and first lit in November 1717. The lighthouse was owned by his family and became the most profitable lighthouse in England and Wales because of tolls raised from passing ships. Trinity House became desperate to buy the lighthouse in 1836 but Trench's descendants, refused to negotiate. When he died, compensation was decided by the court, which awarded his daughter the vast sum of £444,984, equivalent to £22 million pounds today!

Continue along the path, towards the sheer cliffs of Gogarth and the buildings on North Stack headland in the distance.

Head downhill, taking care as the drops are sheer and the cliffs are unprotected. Keep going along the main track, which is rocky with small steps.

At the fork in the tracks, just before it gets very narrow, turn right to hit a broader concrete path. Turn left along this path.

The "drumskins" to your left are microwave communication links to Ireland, and there are also 3 radio masts on this headland.

4. At the radio station buildings, turn left and follow the path around the little brick building to join a tarmac track.

Turn left along this track for about 10m and then immediately right following a broad gravel track.

Ahead and to your left is Holyhead Mountain, which is topped by an Iron Age hill fort, Caer-y-Twr, which dates back to 1000 BC.

At a junction of three tracks, go straight ahead, to the right of the post marked with an arrow. Continue along this gravel path and take the second turn on your right to follow a narrow gravel path through heather.

5. Head along the path between two walls. The path broadens out between gorse bushes and continues behind farm buildings. Bear right to join a track leading from the farm.

Look left here for views along the southern coast of Holy Island and Anglesey.

Continue along the track past another house until you reach the road.

Below you and to your left, just after the wall ends, you can see the outlines of the Ty Mawr huts, one of the best known early settlements in Anglesey. The settlement was lived in sporadically from the Stone Age up until the 6th century AD. There are ten large round huts, from the Iron Age, with the low stone walls clearly visible. They would have originally been capped with thatched conical roofs. These were houses, with a hearth in the centre of the floor and sleeping and storage around the outer edge. Rectangular buildings also present are thought to have been workshops.

Turn left along the road to return to the car park and visit the huts. Access to the huts is free and the site is suitable for pushchairs. The entrance is opposite the car park.

In the area

South Stack Lighthouse is set in a spectacular cliff top location on Ynys Lawd near Holyhead. First lit in 1809, the lighthouse is a beacon to ships crossing the Irish Sea between Holyhead and Dublin and Dun Laoghaire. To access the lighthouse, there are more than 400 steps to climb down (and back up!), so take the papoose. You can visit the engine room and climb to the light chamber at the top of the lighthouse, and there are exhibitions on the lighthouse, the geology and birds of the area. Open Easter – September. (01407 763207)

Breakwater Country Park, Holyhead, is situated in a 106 acre former quarry and is near Holyhead breakwater, one of the longest in the world. There are waymarked walks through the park or you can wander freely. The terrain is varied and includes fields, a lake and the rocky coast where you can look out for the seals, who are regular visitors.

Walk 10: Carmel Head

Allow: *1 hour 45 minutes*

Carmel Head forms the north-west tip of Anglesey, and its peaceful isolation makes it a unique place. There are religious connections with the area; there used to be a church on the headland and the farm you walk past is called Mynachdy, which translates as monastery. The headland is also famous for numerous shipwrecks, due to the strong currents between the islands of the Skerries and West Mouse, and it is a good place for spotting seabirds, seals and porpoises.

The paths are easy and this is a great walk for a sunny day as there are breathtaking views. On a clear day you will be able to see across to the Skerries and, if you are lucky, all the way over to the Isle of Man. So if the weather is good make sure you take a picnic along and sit and enjoy the panorama from this wonderful viewpoint.

Map: Ordnance Survey 1:25000 Explorer OL262 – grid reference 317926

Distance: 3½ miles (5.5 km)

Getting there: Leave the A5025 at Tregele and drive out towards the coast passing Cemlyn Nature Reserve on your right. Once past the nature reserve keep going until you come to a sharp bend in the road with a National Trust sign on the wall 'Ty'n Llan and access to Mynachdy'. Park in the grassy lay-by next to the sign.

Leave the lay by and walk along the footpath which passes through a metal gate with a wooden sign 'Hen Felin' on it. Go past the house to your left and up the grassy track. Lift the pushchair over the locked gate with an adjoining ladder style. Walk straight across the field to the next gate alongside the telephone lines. Go through the gate and continue down the track towards the farm.

The large farm is called Mynachdy which means monastery. The house dates back to the late 1600s.

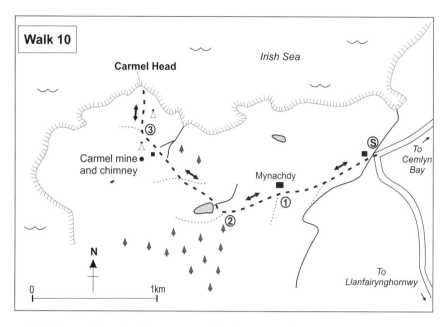

1. Go through a third gate into the farm yard and continue straight ahead to the right of the stable block (blue doors).

Head uphill along the rocky track to another gate (marked with 'dogs to be kept on a lead'). Go through the gate and continue along the track to a further gate on the rise just before a plantation.

To your right you should be able to see a white beacon for shipping directions.

2. Continue along the track towards the plantation. As the track forks alongside the plantation follow the yellow arrow along the right-hand path. Follow the track round the small lake, uphill and round the end of the lake to a gate with an adjoining ladder stile.

Go through the gate, bear to the left of a gorse covered mound and head diagonally across the field towards a gate in the wall. Go through the gate (yellow arrow) and follow the path diagonally

On the way to Carmel Head

right between a wall and a rocky outcrop. Do not continue along the broad muddy track.

Follow the broad grassy track around the hillside towards a ruined building alongside one of the day markers, ignoring smaller paths.

You will now be able to see the beacon on West Mouse Island (Maen-y-Bugael). There are also two day markers (shipping markers) on Carmel Head (Trwyn-y-Gader), the headland in front of you. These markers are used by boats heading towards Liverpool so that they know when to turn in along the coast.

Follow the track to the right of the building, through a gate. Straight ahead is a great view of the islands, The Skerries, with their red and white striped lighthouse, and on a clear day you may also be able to see the Isle of Man.

The buildings are the remains of Carmel Copper Mine, also known as Gader Mine. Mineral veins rich in copper, tin, calamine and zinc were found on the headland and several trial shafts were sunk to explore the vein, which stretch for about 300m. On the site you can see a rickety chimney and several pits and foundations, thought to be the remains of an engine house. There is also a row of four ruined buildings, which were probably housing and workshops.

3. Head downhill towards the other day marker. Pass the marker and continue down to the headland. This is the turning point for the walk, so once you have explored or had a picnic simply return along the route you came.

In the area

Llynnon Mill, Llanddeusant, (01407 730797) is the only working windmill in Wales. Watch the miller unfurl the sails and stone-grind flour from grain. There is a café in the neighbouring building serving traditional food and snacks with craft shops downstairs. Picnic area, toilets and disabled facilities. Open Easter – September.

Howell Mill was the last working watermill in Wales, left over from when Anglesey produced vast quantities of barley and oats. There has been a mill on this site for 650 years. The mill you see today was extended in 1850 and is run by an overshot waterwheel. Open Easter – October, no facilities.

Walk 11: Cemaes Riverside

Allow: 45 minutes

Cemaes is a picturesque village on the north coast of Anglesey and is the most northerly village in Wales! It is located in an area of outstanding natural beauty with stunning rugged coastline and two pleasant, sandy beaches separated by the Victorian harbour and the Afon Wygr.

Unfortunately, the coastal path in this area is too steep and with too many sheer drops to be pushchair friendly, so this easy walk takes you down a hidden river bank beneath the village. The path takes you to the old brickworks, or you can simply wander by the peaceful river and picnic on its bank.

Map: Ordnance Survey 1:25000 Explorer OL262 – grid reference 375937

Distance: 1½ miles (2 km)

Getting there: Park in the beach car park in Cemaes; fee in the tourist season. There are toilets and a kiosk in the car park (closed out of season). A leaflet on other walks around the area is available from the Heritage Centre in the High Street.

From the car park, head back towards the town along a small path to the right of the attendant's hut, marked by an arrow with a wheelchair symbol. Pass a seating area on your right, with nice views of the harbour.

> The harbour seen today was built in the early 1800s, after the earlier pier, built by fisherman, was destroyed in a storm in 1828. Though hard to believe today, Cemaes was once a thriving shipbuilding port, producing ships up to 400 tons. Trade included bricks from the nearby brickworks and ochre from Parys Mountain (Walk 12) as well as limestone and grain.

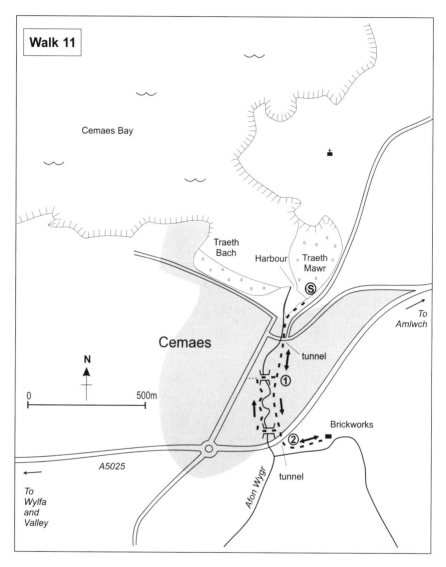

Follow the path round to the left along the riverbank, and through a tunnel passing under the road.

The footpath is an old tramway, leading from the harbour to the brickworks at the end of the walk. Look out for evidence of the original sleepers and rails.

Cemaes harbour

1. At the first junction of paths, continue straight on along the left riverbank. At the next T-junction, turn right following the sign to "Gwaith Bricks 200m". Turn immediately left to walk through the corrugated metal tunnel under the main road.

2. Continue following the path round to the left (don't go up the flight of steps) and follow it to the brickworks, where there is an information board.

Cemaes Brickworks was built in 1907 by Lady Sarah Hughes-Hunter due to the expansion in building for the tourist industry. The brickworks were only operational until the outbreak of the first world war. When working, the kiln was constantly lit and the brick manufacture took place in a series of parallel tunnels divided into smaller chambers.

Return to the metal tunnel and, once through, turn left across the wooden bridge, watching out for damaged slats. Where the path forks, turn right to follow the riverbank.

Cross a second bridge and join a concrete path. At the next fork, go over the wooden bridge, not up the steps, to rejoin the path you started on.

Just by this bridge is a pleasant grassy area ideal for picnics!

Turn left and follow the path back through the tramway tunnel to the beach car park and your car.

In the area

Wylfa Power Station Visitor Centre, near Cemaes, contains an exhibition on nuclear power and electricity. The displays are well thought-out, fun and interactive, and particularly aimed at children. There is a café and shop and the surrounding grounds have a nature trail with a guide leaflet available in the centre. (01407 711400)

Moelfre Seawatch commemorates life above and below the sea. You can climb on board a lifeboat and have a go at the controls while learning about the bravery of the crews. There is a remote controlled camera to view the coastal scenery and you can discover the vast array of life to be found beneath the sea. (01248 410277)

Walk 12: Parys Mountain Copper Trail, Amlwch

Allow: 1 hour 30 minutes

Parys Mountain is located just outside Amlwch on the north coast of Anglesey and has a history of copper mining dating back to the Bronze Age, 3500 years ago. Most copper was produced in the 18th and 19th centuries following the Great Discovery of 2nd March 1768 when Roland Pugh found a mass of copper ore near the surface. In its heyday, Parys Mountain was the largest exporter of copper in the world, and Amlwch was bigger than New York!

This walk takes you around the remains of the mine to see some of the main historic industrial features. Due to the mining, the mountain is now pretty desolate, with limited vegetation. However, the scale of the mining and the different colours of the rocks make this a spectacular location, which was used to film Dr Who! The mine has also featured on Restoration and Extreme Archaeology.

SAFETY: As this is a mine site, there are open shafts (up to 900ft deep) at the surface, mostly fenced, and large pits and pools. Shafts have been known to collapse! Take extreme care to stay on the foot-path and keep children and animals under strict control. Do not cross any fencing and keep away from pools of "water", which are actually highly acidic (pH 1-2).

Map: Ordnance Survey 1:25000 Explorer OL263 – grid reference 437905

Distance: 2 miles (3 km)

Getting there: From Amlwch take the B5111 towards Llangefni. Turn left into the car park signposted "Copper Mine Trail". For further information and a self-guided tour around the route, collect a leaflet (small fee) from the car park. At time of writing, there were plans to have a Guides' hut in the car park, where you will be able to hire the knowledge of Parys Underground Group members for a fully guided tour.

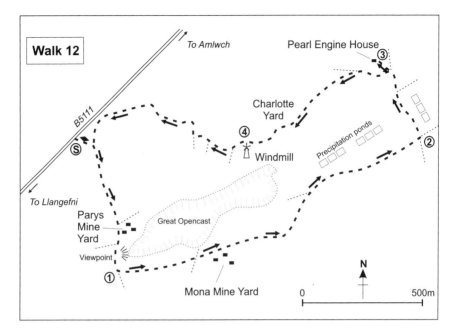

Walk round the metal barrier to follow the white arrow up the stony track. Pass the ponds on your right and continue up the track towards the multicoloured slag heaps.

> Across the ponds you can see the pit-head machinery for the Morris Shaft, which is still operational.

Continue up the track ignoring paths off to the right and left. At the cross-roads, stop to admire the first view of the Great Opencast and look for the buildings of the Parys Mine Yard to your left.

> Parys Mountain was actually two mines, the Parys Mine, here, and the Mona Mine on the opposite site of the opencast pit. This cross-roads was the site of a famous incident in the Parys Mine's history. The miners were paid every three weeks on pay Saturday. This particular Saturday, they met at chapel/smithy; they'd done really well and were owed a lot of money. Word got out that they weren't going to be paid and an angry mob of miners laid siege to the building and blocked gate to the tramway, now visible as a small path. One of the mine owners mounted his horse, opened the gates

and charged through to try and break the siege. But a gust of wind caught the gates and slammed them shut on him and the horse, throwing them both to the ground. The miners rushed forward to rescue the horse! The manager managed to rescue himself, and within 45 minutes the mine owners caved in and the men were paid.

Go straight across the cross-roads, following the arrow, and continue round to the right as the track skirts the Great Opencast. Continue to the viewing platform where you can see the scale of the workings. There is an information board and narration machine.

Until recently, there was a lake located in the pit in front of you. This was full of acidic waters which had been dammed within the mine. There was some concern as to the safety of the concrete dam which had been submerged in the acid for several decades, as nobody knew just how much corrosion the acid had done. If the dam breached, Amlwch would have been flooded with several million gallons of acid, and so it was decided to remove the dam and release the waters under controlled conditions in 2003, opening up more than 5 km of unexplored mine tunnels.

1. Continue along the path, ignoring two turnings to your right, and follow the main path as it curves round to the left. When the path forks, take the left-hand fork to continue straight ahead.

To your right you can see the buildings of the Mona Mine Yard, and on the other side of the opencast you can see the windmill. Keep away from the edge of the opencast as it is not stable.

Continue to the left of two pools, and past a sign marked with a number 2. Meander through the spoil heaps and, at the fork in the path, follow the arrow to the right.

Ravens, choughs and peregrines nest in the crags opposite. The large spoil heap beneath the crags was left by the copper ladies, who you will meet later!

At the next fork, continue straight ahead following the arrow and head downhill.

Just before the next rocky bluff on the right, is a small grassy patch, which is a snail colony of world importance! This was garden waste that was dumped, but due to the acidity of the surrounding ground, the snails have been unable to leave it and so have interbred over several decades, producing a unique community.

Continue to a post marked with a number three, where you come to the precipitation pools used to extract the copper.

The copper was extracted by a displacement reaction with iron. Iron, often scrap metal, was put into the pools, which were filled with copper sulphate solution pumped up from the mine. Because iron is more reactive than copper, it replaces the copper in the solution and pure copper metal is deposited on the floor of the pools. Men were employed to stir the iron in the precipitation ponds to maximise copper precipitation.

Continue downhill towards the lake, noting the red calcining pits to your right. Keep going along the path, passing the lower precipitation pools, to the remains a brick building on your right.

This was an old smelting works and is now a mass of orchids in spring!

2. At the cross-roads at the bottom of the hill, turn left to follow the broad track. Cross a causeway passing the precipitation pools.

The yellow colour in the pools is ochre, and Amlwch Ochre was a very popular paint colour for Edwardian drawing rooms!

Follow the main track as it bends around to the right, ignoring a small right-hand fork. Head for the information board to read about the Pearl Engine House on the hill ahead of you. Continue up the hill towards the engine house, ignoring the white arrow.

The patch of concrete on the floor by the engine house is the cap to a 900ft shaft! This shaft was descended by Michael Faraday during a tour of Wales in 1819.

3. Go back down towards the information board and follow the white arrow to the right. Head up the loose gravel track as it rises

Parys Mountain windmill

uphill ignoring paths to the left and right, and continue around a right-hand bend heading uphill to rest on the bench! Once rested, follow the track round to the left.

Look for the stone circle on the right-hand side opposite a large rocky bluff, which was a present to the mountain from French witches!

Just past the rocky bluff, look for the remains of a brick floor on your right-hand side, which is the site of the Charlotte Yard where the Copper Ladies worked.

The Copper Ladies had the unenviable job of breaking the ore into egg sized pieces for smelting. They used a 4lb hammer and protected their other hand with a chain mail glove. Ore fragments were collected by children.

Continue to the windmill and the trig point to reach the top of the mountain and fantastic views!

The windmill was used for pumping water out of the mine and into the precipitation pools. This was an unusual windmill as it had 5 sails. Wind rather than coal power was used, as wind is free!

4. Go past the windmill and start to head down hill ignoring turns off the main track. Look out for a green grassy patch on your left.

Wherever there were buildings, the miners planted small gardens. The remains of these can be seen today as small, green patches, with grass and some recognisable garden plants.

Follow the arrow round to the right and head down towards the car park. Do not join the main road, but follow the track to the left. At the T-junction, turn right to return to the car park and your car.

In the area

Sail Loft, Amlwch, is a café and industrial heritage centre located in an old sail workshop. The café has an unusual sloping floor, originally to help unroll the massive sails. Downstairs hosts an exhibition on Parys Mountain and Amlwch's past industry. Toilets. (01407 832255)

Swtan, the last thatched cottage on Anglesey can be found in the tranquil village of Church Bay (Porth Swtan). See how traditional croft life was lived and take a stroll on the nearby beach. Cafés and ice cream in the village. Open in summer, Friday, Saturday and Sunday 12pm-4pm.

Walk 13: Red Wharf Bay, Pentraeth

Allow: *1 hour 30 minutes*

This is a nice easy beach walk and is perfect for any season of the year. However, it is especially good in the summer when you can spend some time splashing in the sea as well! There are several options for this walk, some of which are tide-dependant so if you want to spend some time on the beach check the tide times before you go.

Red Wharf Bay is a very shallow bay and at low tide almost 10 square miles of beach is revealed. The area is a haven for a large number of waterfowl and wading birds including shelduck, curlew and oyster-catchers. The beach is backed by salt marshes and sand dunes, which support rare flowers such as the pyramidal orchid.

Map: Ordnance Survey 1:25000 Explorer 263 – grid reference 535799

Distance: 2½ miles (4 km)

Getting there: Leave Pentraeth on the B5109 in the direction of Beaumaris and take the turning on the left signposted to the beach (Traeth). There is a beach side car park at the end of this road.

Turn right out of the car park and follow the footpath, which is marked with yellow arrows (Anglesey Coastal Path) at the edge of the beach so that the sea is on your left.

Simply follow this sandy path along the coast. You will pass over a narrow log bridge and then a reed bed to your right along the way.

1. Just as you pass a small beach hut on the left called Ger-y-Mor you will come to a junction. You now have three choices:

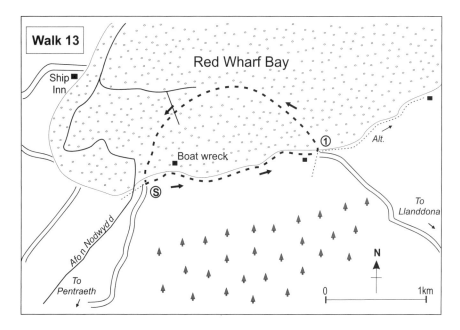

– If the tide is out you can return to the car along the beach as detailed below.

– If the tide is in you will have to return the way you came.

– If you want to extend the walk you can continue along the coastal path to a further car park where there are toilets and a beach café. You could then return along the same path or along the beach depending on the tide.

To return to the car along the beach simply turn left at the junction and head out towards the sea. Bear left so that the sea is on your right and walk back across the sand to the car park.

In the area

Stone Science near Pentraeth provides an unusual experience taking you through the entire history of the earth. Learn how life began and watch it develop through the rock and fossil collections, including dinosaur bones. A must for budding geologists! (01248 450310)

Reservoir Sprogs!

The Ship Inn is located at the west end of Red Wharf Bay, Pentraeth, and is a traditional pub offering excellent food. Child friendly with high chairs and no smoking areas, but no changing facilities. Next to a lovely beach. (01248 852568)

Walk 14: Bwrdd Arthur, Llanddona

Allow: *1 hour 15 minutes*

Bwrdd Arthur (Arthur's Table) is a tranquil limestone plateau to the north of Llanddona. Its location and height (164m) provide some of the best views you'll get in this area; right across Anglesey, out to sea and across to Snowdonia. The hill is capped by a prehistoric hillfort, Din Silwy, which dates back to the Iron Age and which was also used in Roman times (3rd- and 4th-century coins and pottery have been found). The hillfort is surrounded by a protective wall, eight-foot thick, built from limestone slabs stood on edge in 2 to 3 rows filled with rubble. These blocks were obtained by Iron Age man damaging the nearby limestone pavement! The wall is clearly visible from the walk.

The walk takes you on farm tracks and grassy paths, via an old parish church, on a circuit around the hillfort, and you can really appreciate the beauty and tranquillity of the setting. This walk is particularly recommended on a clear day as the views are spectacular!

Map: Ordnance Survey 1:25000 Explorer OL263 – grid reference 587812

Distance: 2 miles (2.5 km)

Getting there: From Llanddona, head north past the pub and the beach turning and follow the signs to Llangoed and Glanrafon. Go past a transmitting mast on your left and round a sharp right-hand bend. About 150m past the bend, park at the triangular junction to a no-through-road, taking care not to block access.

Head along the no-through-road, following the footpath sign and a sign to a church ("eglwys" if the English has been crossed out!).

1. Before you reach the houses to your right, head left through a gateway to view the church.

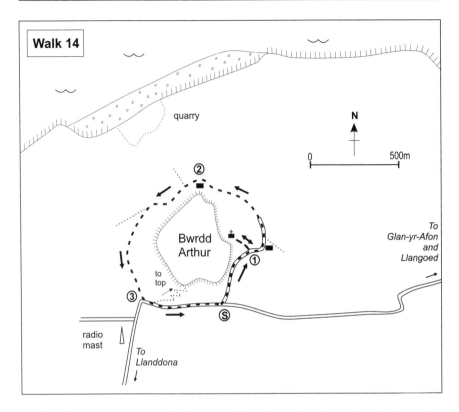

This is the church of Llanfihangel Din Silwy Parish and is dedicated to St Michael. A church at this site is recorded as far back as 1254, but there are no remains present today older than the early 15th century. The nave, bell-cote and chancel are thought to date from this time. The church was restored in the 19th century. Gravestones in the churchyard date back to 1746.

Return to the road and turn left to continue past the houses.

Here, you get views out to see towards the Isle of Man and Lake District. You may also see tankers and the Liverpool-Dublin ferry. To your right you can see Puffin Island (Walk 1) and the Great Orme.

At the junction take the left-hand fork to continue straight ahead. Head towards the house on the hillside.

Llanfihangel Din Silwy church

Look out for the square lime kiln in the field to your left, which can be seen at the base of the limestone escarpment.

2. Follow the track round to the right of the house, between barns and through a gate into a yard. Continue through a second gate, straight ahead and along a grassy (sometimes muddy) track.

Straight ahead you can see Red Wharf Bay (Walk 13) and, in the distance, Point Lynas and its lighthouse.

Take the left-hand, grassy fork off the track, which curves uphill around the hillside. Do not continue along the main track. Go through the gorse, narrow in places (watch out for your baby's eyes!) heading for the mast on the skyline.

As you head around the hill, there are spectacular views across to Snowdonia including (from left to right) the Carneddau, the Glyders and Snowdon itself.

Go through a stone gateway (no gate) and continue between
higher hedges until you reach a gate and stile to the road.

3. Lift over the gate to join the road. Turn left and walk along the
narrow road (look out for traffic!) until you reach the junction
and your car.

Just before the gate, is an access path to the summit marked by a
post with a little brown man, leading up to the southern entrance of
the hillfort. Unfortunately, the path to the top is not pushchair
friendly, but if you take a papoose with you the views are worth the
climb. You can also see the limestone wall to the fort and areas of
intact limestone pavement.

In the area

Beaumaris Courthouse is a fascinating building dating from 1614.
Follow the criminals' footsteps from the prisoners' room to the dock
and learn about some of Anglesey's most notorious criminals. Open
Easter – September, 10.30am – 5pm. (01248 811691)

Red Wharf Bay is a stunning expanse of sandy beach near Pentraeth
on Anglesey's north coast. There are several car parks and a café and
toilets open in season. Dogs are not allowed on certain parts of the
beach from May – September (information in car parks).

Walk 15: Mynydd Bodafon, Bryn Refail

Allow: 1 hour

Mynydd Bodafon is a rocky hill in the north of Anglesey. It is a very tranquil spot with very little traffic noise, which is so hard to escape these days. From the top of the mountain there are spectacular views across Anglesey, the sea and Snowdonia. The scenery is unique in Anglesey.

This is a short but steep walk across access land, initially along tracks by the lake and then up a narrow, rocky and sometimes awkward path up to the summit of the mountain, Yr Arwydd. This route can be slippery in wet weather.

Map: Ordnance Survey 1:25000 Explorer OL263 – grid reference 468850

Distance: 1½ miles (2 km)

Getting there: From Bryn Refail on the A5025, turn south next to the craft centre down a minor country lane. Continue for about 2 miles until the lake comes into view. Park in the lay-by with a bench.

Walk along the road past the lake on your right. Continue past a small field and take the first turning on the right down a track.

Keep following the track round to the right and continue along the lake side. This track can be muddy in wet weather.

1. At the T-junction at the end of the lake, turn left along the track and immediately right down a grassy path past woodland. When the track forks, turn right.

   Look out for tiny Shetland ponies in the field here!

   Continue to a broad, brown track.

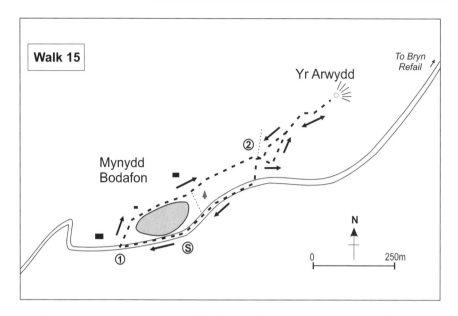

2. Cross the track, go straight through a parking area and up the obvious narrow path which winds up the mountain between gorse bushes. Pass a small path down to the left and continue uphill.

Make sure the pushchair is on a leash at this point and be careful around drops to your right. The path is quite rocky and awkward in places.

As you head towards the summit, when the path forks, take the left branch (easier than the right – they meet up) and continue over several rocky patches until you reach the trig point at a grand height of 178m!

The trig point has orientation markers on each side, naming the main features of the views towards Snowdonia, Great Orme, across Anglesey and back to the lake you passed earlier.

When you have taken in the view, return back down the hill and take the path which forks off to the right and downhill. Continue down this grassy path until it forks, then take the left-hand path back to the parking area (2).

Mynydd Bodafon and lake

Go through the parking area and turn left along the track to the road. Turn right and walk along the road and up the hill to return to your car.

In the area

The Pilot Boat, near Bryn Refail, is a family friendly pub with a good selection of meals. There are changing facilities and even a play bus in the car park!

Benllech Beach is a long, sandy beach with good pushchair access and is popular with families. There are cafés and shops along the promenade and toilets have changing facilities. Picnic area. Dogs are not allowed on certain parts of the beach (information in car parks).

Walk 16: Llyn Cefni, Llangefni

Allow: 2 hours 15 minutes

This large secluded reservoir is sheltered by coniferous forests and provides the perfect setting for a tranquil walk with lots of wildlife to see on the way. The lake is stocked with trout and is popular with anglers. It is also a haven for birds with whooper swans, tufted ducks and many other waterfowl observed here. Red admirals, ringlet and other butterflies are frequently seen along the forest paths and dragonflies can be seen around the lake edge.

This walk takes you along easy paths and forest tracks right around the lake. It can be muddy in wet weather.

Map: Ordnance Survey 1:25000 Explorer OL263 – grid reference 451782

Distance: 4¼ miles (7.5 km)

Getting there: Take the B5111 from Llengefni towards Amlwch. Go through Rhosmeirch and as the road bends to the left you will see a small sign marked with a duck and picnic table. Turn left into the woods and park in the car park.

Follow the track out of the car park and past the metal barrier. Walk along the stone track with the pine forest to your right and open fields to your left.

There are tracks down to the right through the trees to hides on the waters edge for bird watchers.

1. At the end of the track go through the zigzag gate and over a bridge. Follow the track with the reservoir pumping station (pink and beige 1930's buildings) ahead. Follow the zigzag path between the fences down to a second bridge over the reservoir outflow channel (Afon Cefni). Go past the angling hut and red and white post and then turn right down the slate gravel path.

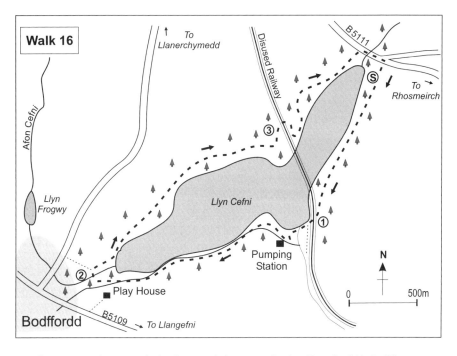

There are plans to link the path here with the Dingle (Walk 17), so in future it may be possible to link the two walks.

Go past the 'no horses' sign, over the little bridge and turn left through the zigzag gates. Follow the flat slate path ahead towards Bodffordd.

Just before you get to Bodffordd you will see an industrial estate on your left. If you fancy a break, the Play House is in this industrial estate. This is a great place for the kids to expend some energy as it has ball pools, soft play areas and a café. There are toddler sessions during the week.

2. Keep following the path as it bends to the right past the industrial estate. Ignore a track heading straight ahead to the road (this eventually leads you to the village and the Play House).

Go along the boardwalk and cross the bridge over the river. Follow the track as it heads through the woods and round the lake.

Dam on Llyn Cefni

3. At the end of the main track take the small path straight ahead which veers to the left into the woods. Cross the disused railway and on the other side go up through a gap in the fence to the right of the large gate and then continue along the woodland path to the right.

Turn left at the junction in the track and walk along the edge of the lake. As you emerge from the woods at a turning circle follow the broad track ahead.

You will now be able to see the bird hides across on the other side of the lake.

Continue along the track through the Christmas trees and when you reach the end go through the black and yellow striped barrier. Turn right onto the road being very careful for traffic (if there are two of you it is possible to cut right onto a small grassy track before the road and over a bridge with a couple of very steep steps on either side). Follow the road (or grassy track) back to the car park.

In the area

Play House (Ty Chwarae) in Bodffordd provides kiddie fun with a large, soft adventure playground including ball pools, cargo nets, slides and much more. There is a separate, enclosed tots' area and a café for parents with a good view over the play area. Changing facilities. (01248 751444)

Oriel Ynys Mon, Llangefni, is a modern exhibition centre, featuring the history and culture of Anglesey. Seasonal exhibitions and a permanent children's activity corner, with plenty for the little ones to do and discover. Café, craft shop, toilets and changing facilities. (01248 724444)

Walk 17: The Dingle (Nant-y-Pandy), Llangefni

Allow: *1 hour*

The Dingle nature reserve is a 25 acre wooded valley in the middle of Llangefni. This steep sided gorge was formed by glacial meltwater and the River Cefni now flows along its base.

The Dingle has recently been regenerated with 650m of boardwalk with footbridges, wooden sculptures, benches and picnic tables. The area is abundant with wildlife. Trees include oak, ash, wild cherry and sycamore and on the woodland floors are ferns, mosses and blue-bells, wood anemones and wild daffodils in spring. There are also abundant birds, and you might even be lucky enough to see a kingfisher

Map: Ordnance Survey 1:25000 Explorer OL263 – grid reference 456758

Distance: 1¾ miles (2.5 km)

Getting there: Park in the pay and display car park in the centre of Llangefni. There are picnic tables next to the car park.

Head out of the far side of the car park and go past a wooden sculpture. Go onto the boardwalk and past the information board. Go up the left-hand side of the river following the boardwalk sign. Do not go over the first bridge.

Go under the railway bridge and follow the boardwalk up the river bank. Ignore the next path up to the left and continue along the boardwalk.

Keep a look out for the wooden sculptures. You should have just passed a large pinecone on your left! There are benches along the route so plenty of opportunities to stop for a break.

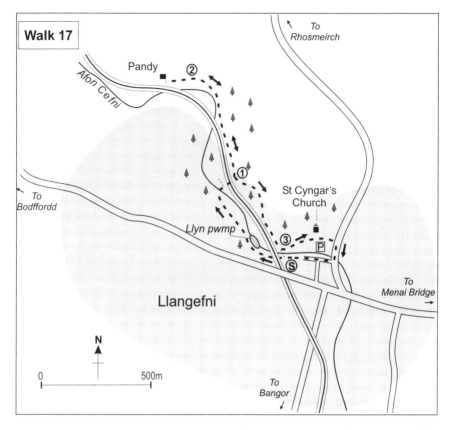

Pass Llyn Pwmp on your right and continue along the boardwalk. Cross over the river and then straight ahead (the left-hand path simply takes you to a viewpoint at present).

1. Go back under the railway and past a red corkscrew sculpture. At the end of the boardwalk you will come to a broad woodland path. Turn left following the signs for woodland walk.

   Follow the path up the hill to a rocky outcrop and then down the other side as it bends to the left. This brings you back to the riverside path (the river is now on your left) which you follow until you see a white house (Pandy).

2. The woodland walk ends at this house so turn around and retrace

your steps back to the boardwalk (there are plans for extending this section of the reserve to link with Llyn Cefni (Walk 16), so it maybe possible to go further in the future).

Sculpture in the Dingle

When you get back to the boardwalk continue straight ahead towards Llangefni with the river on your right (don't turn right onto the boardwalk).

Pass a bench and another sculpture of a beechnut. If you look closely at the benches you can see that they also have carvings on them.

3. Go up the hill, down the other side and past the weir. Go straight on when you see the bridge to your right (this is the shortcut back to the car park). Ignore the path up to the left to Coed Plas as it is too rough.

Turn right and down the boardwalk and pass another bench and sculpture of an Indian. This brings you out to another car park.

To get back to your car, walk through the car park and turn right on to the road. Turn immediately right again and continue straight ahead when the road bends round to the left. This brings you back to the first car park and your car.

In the area

Henblas Country Park (www.parc-henblas-park.co.uk) in the centre of Anglesey provides all weather fun for all the family. Visit the sheep, bunnies and ducks, the indoor and outdoor adventure playgrounds, crazy golf, bouncy castles, face painting and much, much more. Café and picnic areas. Easter – September (closed Saturdays).

The Marquess of Anglesey's Column, Llanfairpwllgwyngyll, is a 27m high pillar of limestone set in woodland. It was built in 1816 and is topped by a bronze statue of the first Marquess. For a small fee you can climb the 115 steps to the balcony for a fantastic view over the surrounding area.

Walk 18: Vaynol Estate, Bangor

Allow: 1 hour 15 minutes

The Vaynol Estate (Faenol in Welsh) consists of 1000 acres of parkland on the shores of the Menai Straits between Caernarfon and Bangor. The original hall was Mediaeval and belonged to a wealthy and powerful Tudor family called Williams who first created the estate. In 1756 William III gave the estate to the Assheton Smiths, who also owned the slate quarries at Llanberis. They built themselves a new manor house and laid out landscaped parkland in the grounds. Today, the park has several owners, and the estate is home to a conservation centre for historic buildings in the area. It also hosts major events such as an annual festival starring the Welsh baritone, Bryn Terfel, and the 2005 National Eisteddfod.

This is a lovely walk around National Trust land across open parkland and through woodland with views across the Straits. The stile can easily be avoided to give you a slightly shorter, but still lovely, walk. Wellies are advisable in winter as it gets very muddy. Please note that dogs must be kept on a lead and livestock must not be disturbed.

Map: Ordnance Survey 1:25000 Explorer 263 – grid reference 535698

Distance: 2½ miles (4 km)

Getting there: From the A55, follow the signs to Parc Menai. Turn onto Parc Menai industrial estate and drive down Ffordd y Parc. Turn left after the trees down Ffordd y Plas and continue past a technical centre on the right and the old Vaynol Estate buildings on your left. At the end of the tarmac continue straight ahead, past a "ramp" sign on the left and through a gateway with a green sign to "Glan Faenol". Park in the National Trust car park at the end of the track (car park closed after 5.30pm and there is no pedestrian access after dusk). There is a picnic area here with a map and information board about the estate.

Go through the gateway at the end of the car park to the left of the picnic site. Go down the hill (can be muddy) and through a second

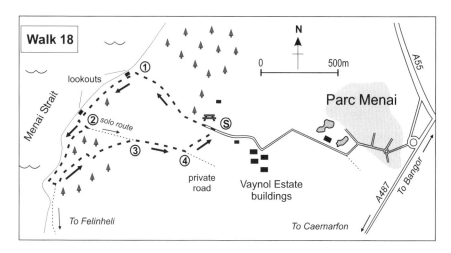

gateway. Walk straight across the field towards the Straits and a wooden viewing platform.

1. Turn left through a small gate to access the viewing platform, then walk along with the wall on your right. You'll have to cross several plank bridges over boggy stretches – these are too narrow for all wheels and "wheelbarrowing" is the easiest way across! Continue past a high bench at a great lookout point across the Straits.

   There are lovely views over the Menai Straits from this walk and you can see Plas Newydd on Anglesey, on the opposite shore. Plas Newydd is the home of the Marquess of Anglesey and parts of the house and the grounds are open to the public.

   Go through a narrow gateway (next to another lookout point) and turn left to walk back up the field with a wire fence on your right. This path takes you away from the Straits and can be a little bumpy in places.

2. Go over a small bridge to a kissing gate on the right part way up the field. The gate is too narrow to push through but it is possible to lift the pushchair over it or over the fence to the side of it.

   If you are solo or want to avoid the kissing gate, continue up the

Plas Newydd from the Vaynol Estate

field with the fence and woodland to your right At the top of the field, go through a gate which brings you to the metal gate at 3.

Follow the path straight ahead through the coniferous woodland on the other side of the gate. The path eventually brings you out onto a broad track, where you turn left.

3. The track takes you up to a large, green metal gate. Go through the gate (or one of the large kissing gates to either side) and continue up the track past a bench on your left.

There are several benches along this track if you want a break and there are views down the hill to Plas Newydd, the Marquess of Anglesey's Column and the Menai Straits.

4. At the next gateway (marked Vaynol Hall Residents only) turn left to walk between wooden and wire fences. Go through the wide kissing gate and turn immediately left through a gate with adjoining cattle grid back into the National Trust car park.

In the area

Greenwood Forest Park (www.greenwoodforestpark.co.uk) is a great day out with plenty to do for the whole family. There is a toddlers' village, little green run slide and a great sand play area. They can also meet bunnies, drive mini tractors and much more!

Penrhyn Castle, near Bangor, (www.nationaltrust.org.uk) is a 19th-century castle built by the Pennant family, who owned the slate quarries at Bethesda. The castle is Victorian "nouveau-riche", with elaborate stonework and décor, and stands in 45 acres of gardens. There is a tea room, train museum, doll museum and art gallery.

Walk 19: Lon Eifion and Y Foryd, Caernarfon

Allow: *2 hours 30 minutes*

This walk begins along Lon Eifion, one of several recreational routes in Gwynedd, which, at its start, follows the Welsh Highland Railway south from Caernarfon. The route then leaves Lon Eifion to follow pleasant country lanes and off-road tracks to meet the Menai Straits near Foryd Bay south of Caernarfon.

The route is on easy terrain: a long walk suitable for small babies in pushchairs. Views of the Menai Straits are spectacular and as you approach Caernarfon on the return leg, you are rewarded by one of the best views of Caernarfon Castle.

Map: Ordnance Survey 1:25000 Explorer OL263 – grid reference 480625.

Distance: 4½ miles (7.5 km)

Getting there: Follow the signs to the Welsh Highland Railway in Caernarfon. Park in the station car park or by the roadside. If no space, the station is only 5 minutes walk from the large car park near the slate quay. This walk can also be done from the train.

Walk along the road by the railway until you come to a sign to "Lon Eifion". Go through the gate and beneath the bike to walk along the path by the railway.

Follow the railway under a footbridge and a road bridge. Continue on the right-hand side of the railway when you come to a crossing, do not cross the tracks. Go over the river, visible to your right, and under a second road bridge. At the next railway crossing, continue straight ahead beside the track.

The Welsh Highland Railway, at time of writing, consists of two separate halves – Caernarfon to Rhyd Ddu and Porthmadog to

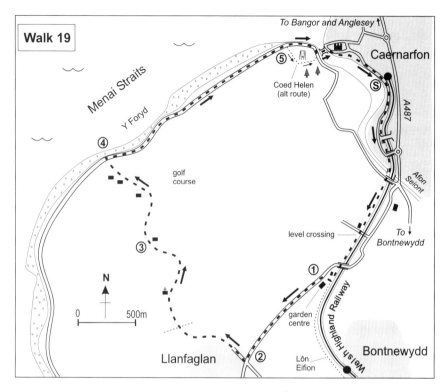

Pen-y-Mount, just outside the town. Work is currently underway, to restore the entire route from Caernarfon to Porthmadog via Beddgelert. Work is scheduled for completion in 2008, with passenger services starting 2009. So, in the near future, this walk will tie in with a day trip from Porthmadog (Walk 30), or even Blaenau Ffestiniog!

1. Go under a third road bridge and turn right immediately after a white house. Go through the gate and go straight ahead to meet the road. Cross the road and turn left to walk along the road, watching out for traffic. Go past Fron Goch garden centre and continue along the road until you come to Llanfaglan village.

2. Pass the village sign and turn right at the cross roads to walk down a narrow lane. Go past the phone box and continue along the road and uphill, past a converted chapel. As you start to

descend downhill, there are good views across the Menai Straits to Anglesey. At the end of the metalled lane, go through a gate and continue down a broad track heading towards a large farm, following the public footpath sign.

Straight ahead is a good view of Abermenai Point and Fort Belan. Abermenai Point is the spit of sand sticking out into the straits, and marks the narrowest point of the straits. Across from Abermenai Point is Fort Belan, built in 1775 by Thomas Wynne (later the 1st Lord Newborough) to fortify this narrow stretch of the straits during the Napoleonic wars. The fort also has a dock and was occupied by the forces during World War II, due to the use of nearby Caernarfon Airport.

3. Once at the farm, turn right and walk through the farmyard. Continue past the barns and go straight ahead through a double gate to follow a grassy track between two hedges.

At the end of the grassy track, turn left, following the yellow footpath sign, through a narrow metal gate. Pass a house on your left and continue through a wide gate to walk down a neat, grassy driveway past two more houses. Caernarfon golf course is on your right so beware of flying golf balls!

4. Go through the gate at the end of the drive, carefully cross the road and turn right to walk along the road by the Foryd shore back to Caernarfon. After about a mile, Caernarfon Castle comes into view.

Coed Helen Park on your right is worth a visit as it has a good children's playground, picnic area and toilets (locked out of season).

5. Once you've finished in the park, return to the road and cross over the Aber Swing Bridge to the other side of the Afon Seiont, or follow the path past the playground to the road and head down to the bridge

To your right, from the bridge, you can see the slate quay, which

Caernarfon Castle

once thronged with ships transporting Snowdonia roofing slates all over the world.

Once over the bridge, turn right to walk in front of the castle, following the green signs to the Welsh Highland Railway. (If you want to have a look around Caernarfon, turn left and through the gateway to get to the Castle and the town centre.)

Caernarfon Castle, built between 1283 and 1327, is the greatest of Edward I's castles in Wales. Look out for the unusual octagonal towers capped by eagles, with coloured banding in the stone, designed to be reminiscent of Constantinople. As the importance of the area diminished, the full design was never completed and you can see the unfinished Queen's Gate, suspended half way up a wall, as you walk along the quayside.

Pass the car park and bear right, towards the Oriel Llywelyn

Gallery and the grey limestone harbour offices dated 1840. Cross the road at the roundabout and follow the footpath back to the station to find your car.

In the area

Caernarfon Castle (www.cadw.wales.gov.uk) is one of the world's greatest medieval castles and certainly the most striking medieval monument in Wales. The castle was constructed by Edward I not only as a military stronghold but also as a royal palace. Its unique polygonal towers and colour banded walls as well as its sheer size make it a spectacular place to visit. The castle is open all year except December and January.

The Fun Centre (Y Hwylfan), Caernarfon, offers a variety of fun activities for all the family – ball pools, rope bridges, slides, cargo nets and much more. As well as games for the Big Kids, there are two large play areas for under-5s with seating. There is also a café and baby changing facilities. (01286 671911)

Walk 20: Glynllifon Country Park, Caernarfon

Allow: 1 hour 30 minutes

Glynllifon Country Park is a Grade 1 listed garden offering up to eight miles of country pathways. The park was laid out in the 18th and 19th centuries by the Newboroughs (formerly the Wynne family), and nestles in the valley of the Afon Llifon. As well as the mansion house, the historic home of the Newboroughs, there are gardens, woodland, an arboretum, follies and water features. Glynllifon was opened as a Country Park in 1991 to enable visitors to appreciate the historic gardens.

This walk takes you on a pushchair-friendly route to visit the main features of the gardens. As you wander the grounds, you will come across several follies, including the Mill, Hermitage and Children's Mill. Once you've finished, you might want to pay a visit to the arts and crafts centre in the old workshops, or have a cuppa in the excellent café.

Map: Ordnance Survey 1:25000 Explorer OL254 – grid reference 454555

Distance: 2½ miles (4 km)

Getting there: Follow the A499 from Caernarfon to Pwllheli. Glynllifon Country Park is well signposted on your left-hand side. Follow the drive to the car park. Leaflets showing more details of the footpaths are available from the ticket office.

Leave the ticket office and turn right to head down towards the mill, following signs to "Melin Glanrafon and Historic Gardens. Follow the wheelchair sign to avoid a flight of steps by the mill. Go up the drive signposted "Llwybrau/Walks" with a yellow footprint.

At the double gate turn left through the fence and along the path through the trees following the river.

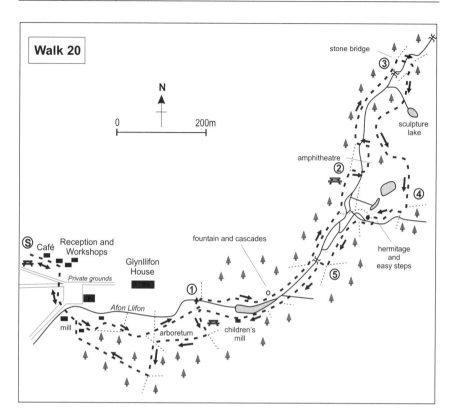

The trees are labelled as part of the Tree Trail, leaflets available from the ticket office.

Go through the fences and cross the road, looking out for traffic.

To your left is the main façade of Glynllifon House, the centre of which is dominated by a six-column portico. Lord Newborough built the house and estate in the middle of the 19th century, along with stables, the entrance arch and two lodges. The mansion is now a college of further education but retains many of its original features, such as the dramatic portico, decorative plaster covings, ornate ceiling roses, stained glass windows and a Victorian conservatory. The cellars are home to a large colony of the rare lesser-horseshoe bat.

Go through the fences opposite and continue along the woodland path past a bench. Continue past a giant redwood and a huge monkey puzzle tree, where you will see a pleasant picnic area on your right. Turn left at the monkey puzzle tree and then right to follow the yellow footprint sign just before you reach the river.

Pass a bench and continue into the Arboretum, where the path is lined with bamboo. Continue through the tall noble firs to the river.

Arboretums were very fashionable in the 19th century, with the expansion of global exploration. Trees were grown from seeds or plants collected all over the world by explorers and the rare trees were a source of competition amongst the nobility.

1. Cross over the river via a green metal bridge and turn right along the bank, heading towards the fountain in the centre of a large expanse of lawn.

Go past the cascades to the fountain straight ahead of you. Continue past the fountain and along the broad woodland track.

The fountain was one of three built in the 1840s in the dingle east of the house. The nearby cascades are older, dating back to the 1820s and 1830s and comprise a stepped series of waterfalls descending to the stream.

At the next junction, continue straight ahead following the blue signs to the Amphitheatre. Continue along this path, looking out for more cascades and the Hermitage to your right.

2. Go to a second picnic area and cross the river by the first wooden bridge to visit the Amphitheatre. Carefully walk along the front of the Amphitheatre (the drop is not protected) and cross the two bridges back to the path, via Yew Tree Island.

The Amphitheatre is an open-air theatre made of local slate is the venue for summer concerts and plays. There are two viewing towers and stepped seating. You can see the stage across the river on Yew Tree Island. This island was man-made and planted in the

1820s with Irish yew trees to form arches. Look out for the mosaic on the island, made from coloured pebbles depicting the Newborough coat of arms.

Water feature in Glynllifon!

Turn right to follow the signs to Nant Ynysoedd (Valley of the Islands). Continue until you come to a stone bridge.

3. Cross the river by the stone bridge and head straight on up the hill towards the sculpture and waterfall.

The sculpture celebrates the quarrymen's strike of 1900. Just past the sculpture is a small lake with an arm sticking out of the water!

At the lake, turn right and follow the signs towards the Hermitage. Continue along the high path by the fence. There are 2 steps down and a total of 9 easy steps up. Go over the wooden footbridge (1 shallow step at either end) and continue along the path.

4. Go through the gap in the wall and turn right. Look out for the little blue tree trail signs by the path side to confirm your route! Don't cross the footbridge, but turn right down a very easy flight of steps to the hermitage.

To visit the Hermitage you'll need to park the pushchair as the access steps are steep. This is a gothic folly built around 1825, and was allegedly the home of a paid hermit, until he was sacked for spending all his time and money at the pub! The hermitage was later converted into a chapel and the family pet cemetery can be found nearby.

Cross over the hump-backed bridge and turn right to walk down the opposite stream bank. Continue along the path, turning left; do not go down the steps to the next bridge.

5. At the next junction, turn right down towards the small stone bridge. Turn left just before you get to the bridge to walk along the riverbank. Continue along the metalled path by the cascades, where there is a good view across to the house. Go over a bridge in front of the Children's Mill and continue straight on back into the Arboretum.

The Children's Mill folly is a Nymphaeum which was allegedly inhabited by "fairies, threatening snakes, huge snails, monstrous toads and gigantic fungi, which crop up unexpectedly from among the tall graceful ferns".

At the next junction, turn left away from the bridge and walk through the trees. Turn right past tree number 47 and continue to come out at the Cromlech picnic site.

Turn left following the bird and cromlech sign and continue until you come to some charcoal kilns. Turn right at the charcoal kilns and walk down the path, round the double gates and follow the road back to the garden entrance and café.

In the area

Gypsy Wood Park (www.gypsywood.co.uk) is the largest LGB garden railway in Wales. There are lots of miniature animals, a touch and smell garden, wetland walk and small children's play area. It is open between Easter and mid September 10.30am-5pm.

Caernarfon Air World (www.airworld.co.uk) offers scenic flights over the North Wales coast and mountains, and an Aircraft Museum including combat planes, relics from wartime wrecks and an interactive section where you can take over the pilot's controls. Café.

Walk 21: Bwlch-yr-Eifl, Llithfaen

Allow: 1 hour 30 minutes

The former quarry village of Porth-y-Nant nestles at the foot of Nant Gwrtheyrn, a beautiful valley near Llithfaen. The village was built in 1853 and comprised 24 workmen's houses, a foreman's house, co-op shop, a bakery, a chapel and a mansion. It was very inaccessible so all goods were carried in by sledge. The last inhabitants left in 1959. The village was adapted to be the National Welsh Language Centre in 1978.

This walk takes you along the top of the valley along a pass below Yr Eifl (564m). Though it's a long uphill stretch, you are rewarded by beautiful views down the valley and over Snowdonia, Anglesey and the Lleyn Peninsula at the top. And it's all downhill on the way back!

Map: Ordnance Survey 1:25000 Explorer 254 – grid reference 352440

Distance: 2½ miles (4 km)

Getting There: Take the road from Llithfaen on the B44171 towards Nant Gwrtheyrn Welsh Language and Heritage Centre (signposted) and park the car in the first car park on the left-hand side.

Turn right out of the car park and walk up the road for a short distance.

1. Turn left up the broad gravel track signposted as a public bridleway and the Lleyn Coastal Path.

   The hill straight ahead of you is Yr Eifl (the Rivals). Yr Eifl Quarry can be seen on the hill to your left. You will soon see the sea down on your left past the valley, Nant Gwrtheyrn, and the buildings down in the bay are the National Welsh Language and Heritage Centre (Canolfan Genedlaethol Iaith). Holyhead Mountain can be seen across the water.

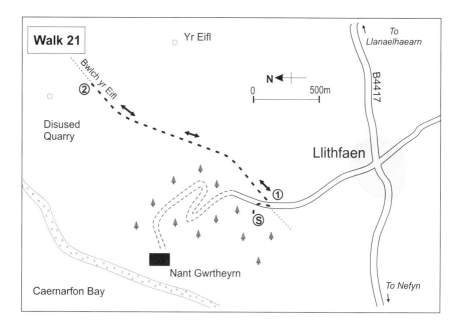

Nant Gwrtheyrn Welsh Language and Heritage Centre allows visitors to discover more about the Welsh language and culture, and runs residential courses for learners of Welsh. Caffi Meinir serves light meals on weekdays and Sunday lunches, and there is a footpath down to the beach (just pushchairable!). The centre also sells leaflets of more walks around the valley (not pushchair friendly). The heritage centre is closed at weekends. For more information see nantgwrtheyrn.org.

2. Simply continue walking up the steady incline until you reach the top of the pass, Bwlch-yr-Eifl, where you will get a stunning view over the mountains of Snowdonia with Snowdon directly ahead of you.

   There are fantastic views up the coast to Anglesey and when you turn around you will be able to see along the coast of the Lleyn Peninsular.

   Turn around and retrace your tracks to the car park.

Bwlch-yr-Eifl from Porth Dinllaen

In the area

Glynllifon Park is a craft centre and Grade I listed garden in the grounds of an 18th-century mansion. The gardens have woodland paths and hidden follies and there are family treasure hunts and special events throughout the year. Excellent café, craft workshops, play ground and toilets with changing facilities. 01286 830222

Dinas Dinlle is a prehistoric hillfort south of Caernarfon located next to a long sandy beach with lovely views across to Anglesey. The fort ramparts are easily visible from the approach road and the top is accessed by a flight of steps. The seaward side is slowly being eroded away as it is formed from soft glacial sediment. The village has numerous cafés and beach shops, toilets with changing facilities and a playground.

Walk 22: Porth Dinllaen, Morfa Nefyn

Allow: 1 hour 45 minutes

Porth Dinllaen was a busy port in the 19th century with many sailing ships importing and exporting goods to the isolated Lleyn Peninsular. Heavy shipping traffic in this sheltered harbour made it inevitable that accidents would happen. In 1863, a severe gale swept eighteen ships ashore that had been sheltering in the harbour. The ships were wrecked, but five men, headed by Robert Rees, were able to save 28 sailors from the vessels. A few days later a request was sent to the R.N.L.I. for a lifeboat station to be established in the harbour. This life-boat station was opened in 1864 and has been saving lives ever since. Porth Dinllaen nearly became the main port for Dublin, but in 1810 Holyhead won the vote for Irish Sea traffic.

This pretty village is now protected by the National Trust and with its beach and pub makes the perfect place to visit on a summer's day. The route takes you out on the top of the peninsular to the lifeboat station and then returns through the village and along the beach. So why not relax and spend some time splashing in the sea on your return to the car.

Check the tide times before you go as the beach section of this route is inaccessible at high tide.

Map: Ordnance Survey 1:25000 Explorer 253 – grid reference 281408

Distance: 3 miles (5 km)

Getting there: From the centre of Morfa Nefyn turn down the road, Lon Pen Rhos, towards Porth Dinllaen and park in the first car park, sign-posted Traeth (beach), at the end of the road.

Walk back to the car park entrance where there is a shed and a picnic table. Turn right out of the entrance and walk up the track.

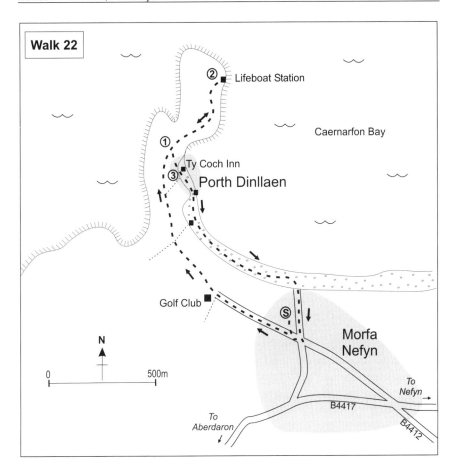

The hills to your right are the Rivals and Garn Boduan is behind you.

Go through the gate and along the path through the golf course. When you come to a junction go straight ahead on the broad gravel track. Continue along this track towards the end of the headland.

Just before you get to the turning point on this track there is a large blow hole to your left. Keep small children away from the blow hole. At the bottom of this blow hole there is an obvious cave entrance, which leads out to the sea.

1. Pass a turning on the right, marked 'no unauthorised vehicles', and a parking area and then go through a gateway.

If you don't want to walk to the end of the headland turn right down the 'no unauthorised vehicles' track to the village of Porth Dinllaen then follow the directions from 3.

Continue up the concrete road, which takes you through an ancient hill fort (partially destroyed by the golf course). When the path forks, turn right along the main track.

Down below you to the right is Porth Dinllaen where there is a pub!

2. Continue along the track, past the small tower and you will arrive at the life boat station. There are a series of small steps to go down to reach this point.

There are great views over the sea to Anglesey from this rocky headland as well as of the Rivals to your right.

Return along the same path until you come to a track on the left, marked 'no unauthorised vehicles', which takes you down to the small village of Porth Dinllaen.

3. The track brings you out behind the Ty Coch Inn.

In the 1920s, the landlady of the Ty Coch Inn, Mrs Jane Jones, was the only female harbourmaster in the whole of the British Isles!

Turn right and walk back to your car along the beach (if the tide is in you will have to return to the car along the route you came).

As you walk along the beach head for a small house on a rocky outcrop.

As you approach the house you will pass some old sand dunes with lots of burrows within them on your right. Beware, these dunes are unstable.

Take the path that goes behind the house and down onto the next section of beach. Continue across the beach and past the front of

The coast at Porth Dinllaen

the next white house. Keep going until you reach a cluster of houses and where you turn right up the slipway. Go up the hill, past the toilets (locked out of season) and turn right at the end of the road to the car park.

In the area

Inigo Jones Slateworks, near Caernarfon, is a fully operational slateworks where you can watch the craftsmen at work and have a go at your own slate calligraphy. Regular competitions for children. Welsh music-themed café. Open all year (www.inigojones.co.uk).

Antur Waunfawr (www.anturwaunfawr.org) Set up to offer training and experience for people with disabilities, Antur Waunfawr offers a warm Welsh welcome. Explore the park with its eco-cabin, adventure footpaths and children's playground. Visit Ty Capel to learn about the community's history and wildlife in the park. Finish your visit with a meal at the 'Blas-y-Waun' café. Open from 10am – 4pm (5pm in summer). Park always open.

Walk 23: Mynydd Carreg and Whistling Sands, Aberdaron

Allow: 2 hours

Whistling Sands (Porth Oer) is a popular beach between steep grassy headlands. The beach gets its name from the whistling sound the sand makes when walked on. It doesn't always occur, but is an interesting experience when it happens! Allegedly, there is only one other beach in Europe where this happens. The Welsh name, Porth Oer, is not so romantic – "oer" means cold!

The route first takes you round Mynydd Carreg, famous for its deposits of jasper which were quarried in the last century. The site is now access land, owned by the National Trust, and there is a lookout tower on the summit. The track around the mountain is easy going, and the views across the beach and out to sea are spectacular – take a picnic on a sunny day to truly absorb the scenery!

Map: Ordnance Survey 1:25000 Explorer 253 – grid reference 162289

Distance: 3½ miles (5.5 km)

Getting there: From the B4413 between Sarn Meyllteyrn and Aberdaron take the signposted turning towards Whistling Sands. Go past the turning on the right to the Whistling Sands car park and continue slightly further along the road to the Carreg National Trust car park (indicated by a brown National Trust sign).

Go to the far end of the grassy car park and through the kissing gate or adjoining gate. Follow the track as it bears round to the left alongside the wall.

There are lovely views down the peninsular to the hills Mynydd Anelog and Mynydd Mawr.

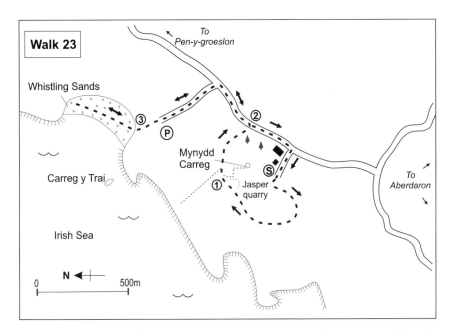

Keep following the track as it bends round to the right and heads out towards the coast.

You will soon see the small island of Carreg-y-Trai and the headland at the far end of Whistling Sands.

Continue along the track, don't go left at any of the gates. At the first junction stay to the right-hand side of the post and continue straight ahead. Go through the next kissing gate or adjoining gate.

To your right there is a lookout tower on the top of the hill, and the remains of a jasper quarry. Jasper is a red semi-precious stone used for decorative purposes. There are several deposits on the Lleyn Peninsula and this deposit, with a variegated red colour, was discovered by Captain Trevethan and was being quarried in 1904. Jasper from Mynydd Carreg is said to have been worked and taken to London.

The lower quarry levels provide a large flat grassy area with lovely coastal views which is ideal for a picnic or play.

For the more adventurous there is a path up to the lookout point which is easily pushchairable. If you don't want to go up to the lookout, skip the next paragraph and follow the directions from 1.

Just past the quarry there is a narrow track up the hill to the right, ignore this and take the second track. This broad track zigzags up the hill and it is then just a short push up a grassy slope to the lookout tower. Once you have admired the view simply retrace you steps back down the hill and turn right onto the main path.

1. Continue along the track and through another kissing gate or adjoining gate. Stay on this track heading towards some trees and when you come round the corner you will see a gate.

   Look out for cows, which are often kept in this field.

2. Go through the gate and turn left onto the road. Walk down the road and take the next left turning which is signposted to Whistling Sands. Follow this road down and past the car park (there is a picnic table here) to the beach.

   There are lovely views out to sea and as you walk down the road you will be able to see the small island of Carreg-y-Trai ahead.

3. Go right down to the end of the road and onto the beach. This is a beautiful spot with lovely sea and coastal views so it is worth spending some time here. Explore the beach, take a dip in the sea or have a picnic. When you are done walk back up the road, past the car park and turn right at the end. Follow the road as it heads gently uphill, past the wood and take the next turning on the right up to the National Trust Carreg car park.

In the area

Bodvel Hall Adventure Park (01758 613733) at Boduan (near Pwllheli) is for families who fancy a spot of fun. The kids can burn up some energy while the adults relax in the grounds. Visit the animal farmyard and see the birds of prey. Mums can take instruction in the off-road driving centre while dads look after the kids in

Whistling Sands

the indoor play area. Relax in the Riverside coffee shop and take a stroll along one of the nature trails. Open Easter – September.

Plas-yn-Rhiw is a small 17th-century mansion with ornamental gardens overlooking Hell's Mouth beach. Woodland walks with picnic area. National Trust shop. Open March – October. (01758 780219)

Walk 24: St Mary's Church and Mynydd-y-Gwyddel, Aberdaron

Allow: 1hour

Mynydd Mawr and Mynydd-y-Gwyddel have been called the Land's End of Wales. They are situated right at the end of the Lleyn Peninsula and on a clear day there is an uninhibited view across Cardigan Bay to the Pembroke Coast. Just off the end of the Peninsula is Bardsey Island (Ynys Enlli), a place of holy pilgrimage for centuries. In the valley between the two mountains at the cliff foot, is a spring, St Mary's Well (Ffynnon Mair) which, in certain tidal conditions, flows with fresh water.

This walk takes you along grassy and rocky paths past ancient remains and up to the top of Mynydd-y-Gwyddel for fantastic views across Bardsey Sound and along the Lleyn coast towards Aberdaron. This is a fantastic, peaceful place for relaxing, playing and picnicking!

Map: Ordnance Survey 1:25000 Explorer 253 – grid reference 142255

Distance: 1½ miles (2.5 km)

Getting there: Follow the road from Aberdaron to St. Mary's Well. Park in the car park (large grassy area) just before the road begins going up hill. There is an information board about the area here.

Walk up to the corner of the field enclosure on the coastal side of the car park and turn left following the fence towards the coast. The hill to your right is Mynydd Mawr. At the far corner of the fence follow the path straight ahead, don't go left round the field.

You will be able to see the stripes in the field below you these are the remains of an ancient farming system. Also in the field below you should be able to make out the outline of a building in the grass. This was "St Mary's Church", said to be a last resting point of pilgrims before they made the dangerous crossing over the

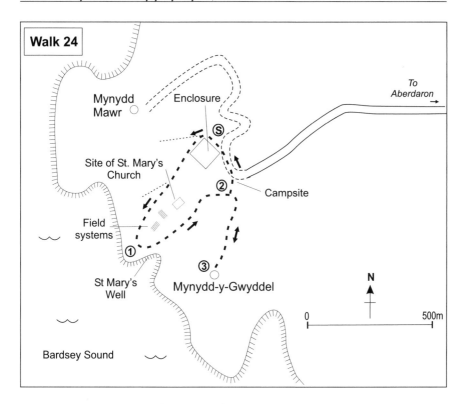

Sound to Bardsey. This route for the pilgrims is unlikely, and drawings of the building indicate it was more likely to have been a house. This interpretation also ties in with the numerous cultivation ridges on the hillside.

1. Walk down the grass slope, past the site of the church and straight out towards the coast. This is a great spot for a picnic but take care of children near the cliff edge.

Ahead is Bardsey Island which can be reached by boat from Aberdaron and Pwllheli in the summer. The ravine to your left is the site of St. Mary's Well. This is not accessible as it involves a steep climb down the ravine.

Once you have spent some time admiring the view follow the path back round to the site of the church. Pass to the right of this

The coast from St Mary's church

site and follow the track to the right and over a small stream. Turn left straight after the stream and walk up towards a stone wall.

2. Turn right at the crossroads next to the stone wall and walk up the hill (Mynydd-y-Gwyddel) ahead of you.

3. The path takes you to the top of the hill from which there are spectacular views along the coast.

   To the left you will be able to see Hell's Mouth and Snowdonia. Ahead you look across Cardigan Bay to the Pembrokeshire Coast. To the right you will be able to see across the Irish Sea and on a clear day you will be able to make out the Irish coastline.

   To return to the car, simply turn around and follow the path back down to the stone wall. Go straight ahead at the crossroads at the corner of the wall. This takes you back to the road, which you then follow as it goes gradually back up hill to the car park.

In the area

Bardsey Island lies off the southern tip of the Lleyn Peninsula and was a place of pilgrimage for many years. Nowadays it is run by the Bardsey Island Trust and day trips are available from Porth Meudwy, near Aberdaron, or Pwllheli, with around 3½ hours to explore the island. Pushchairs can be taken and some of the low level paths are suitable. You can visit the remains of the 13th-century abbey and see Britain's tallest square lighthouse. The coasts are packed with seals and sea birds and Bardsey produce is available in the shop (www.bardsey.org).

Whistling Sands between Aberdaron and Nefyn is a cosy cove with a white sandy beach. It gets its English name from the fact that the sands whistle when walked upon. Beach café and toilets open in season. No dogs.

Walk 25: Mynydd Rhiw

Allow: 2 hours

Mynydd Rhiw is a long, humped hill between Aberdaron and Abersoch. It lies at the western end of Hell's Mouth (Porth Neigwl), a vast sandy beach popular with surfers. On a clear day the views from all sides are stunning – across Hell's Mouth to Abersoch and the mountains of Snowdonia beyond, and north to Anglesey, the Isle of Man and even the Lake District and Ireland!

This walk aims to make the most of these views, but is also very atmospheric on a foggy day! The track across the mountain is good, but there is a lot of up-hill pushing to be done.

Map: Ordnance Survey 1:25000 Explorer 253 – grid reference 237298

Distance: 3½ miles (5.5 km)

Getting there: Drive along the B4413 from Llanbedrog to Botwnnog. Turn left immediately before a chapel at the start of the village. Drive down this road and take the third turning on the left (the first two are no-through roads) which is signposted to Rhiw. Park in the small car park on the right, which is marked with a National Trust sign. (N.B. Do not attempt to go direct from Hell's Mouth, as the road from there to Plas-yn-Rhiw has been destroyed by a landslide.)

Follow the broad stone and dirt track out of the far end of the car park, with fantastic views across Snowdonia to the sea and the Isle of Man. Stay on this main path, ignoring all turnings to the left and right, as it heads uphill and bends round to the left.

As you come to the brow of the hill and the track straightens out, there is a small loop of track to your right. If you head down this, you may be able to make out a couple of small depressions in the ground on your right. These are all that remains of a Neolithic axe factory. The rock for the axes was taken from around a volcanic plug, where the heat baked the surrounding rock making it extremely

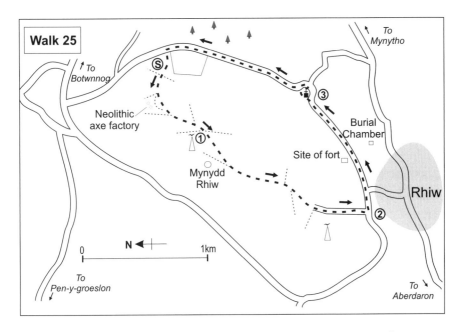

hard. Axes from this site have been found as far away as Gwent in South Wales.

1. Continue straight ahead at the crossroads with the radio masts to your right. As you walk along the track you will see a second track joining from the right and just behind this there is a trig point on the peak. Stay on the main path as it begins to head downhill.

The path soon runs alongside a stone wall on the left and immediately after this the path forks. Stay on the main track, which forks off to the left.

As you continue downhill you will come to the end of the track with another radio mast to your right. Simply continue straight ahead along the tarmac road.

As you walk down the hill you will be able to see along the coast to Aberdaron and Mynydd Mawr to your right. To your left is Hell's Mouth (Porth Neigwl) and the headland near Abersoch.

2. Turn left at the t-junction, walk along the road and take the next

Church on Mynydd Rhiw

turning on the left (do not continue down the road to Rhiw. This road will now take you all the way back to the car park.

There are fantastic views down over Hell's Mouth to your right with Snowdonia in the far distance. As you walk along the road you will soon see a footpath arrow to your right. This is not pushchair friendly but takes you to the site of a burial chamber. On the opposite side of the road is the site of an ancient fort.

3. When you come to a small church you can either follow the road as it curves around the church or go through the small gate into the graveyard (N.B. there are adders' nests in the churchyard!). If you go through the graveyard follow the path round the back of the church and leave by the gate at the other side. Then simply turn left and continue to follow the road.

The large pointed hill straight ahead is Carn Fadryn, another of the Lleyn's Iron Age hillforts. It is also the site of Madryn Castle, an important Welsh castle built in the 12th century. The Madryn estate, at the foot of the hill, is the origin of the name of Puerto Madryn in Patagonia. This is where Welsh settlers first landed in 1865 after a 2 month journey from Liverpool. The settlers had a very tough time, but 20,000 of their descendants are still in Patagonia today and Welsh is still spoken by about 5000 people.

Continue along the road and past a piece of National Trust land (Pen-y-Mynydd) until you see your car in the car park on the left.

In the area

Hell's Mouth (Porth Neigwl) between Abersoch and Aberdaron is a vast beach at the southern end of the Lleyn Peninsula. The sands stretch for 4 miles and so peace and quiet can usually be found. Popular with surfers, but there is a strong undertow. Car parking but no other facilities.

Cilan Riding Centre, near Abersoch, offers cross-country rides round the headland. The riding is suitable for all riders, including novices and children (from 4 years). Riding hats are provided and all rides are escorted. (01758 713276)

Walk 26: Abersoch to Machroes

Allow: 2 hours

Abersoch is a popular seaside village at the southern end of the Lleyn Peninsula. Surrounded by beautiful beaches and tranquil countryside it is the social hub of the area in summer, with pubs and cafés, surf shops, music festivals and surf and sailing competitions.

This is an easy walk across the golf course to the headland at nearby Machroes and back via the beach. There is plenty of opportunity for sandcastle building and picnics so make sure you take the full kit!

Map: Ordnance Survey 1:25000 Explorer 253 – grid reference 314277

Distance: 4 miles (6.5 km)

Getting there: Leave Abersoch and follow the signs for Sarn Bach. Take the first turning on the left and drive down the road until you come to the large beach car park.

Walk back to the entrance of the car park and turn left following the road to the golf club. This road takes you all the way through the centre of the golf course so watch out for flying golf balls!

1. When you reach a fork in the track turn right. Follow this lane straight over a staggered crossroads, past a farm and all the way up into the village of Bwlchtocyn. Turn left at the end of the lane where there is a church on the left. Walk along the road and take the next turning on the left, which is signposted towards Porth Tocyn Hotel.

   You will soon see the first of the coastal views with Abersoch beach directly ahead.

2. Follow the road as it bends to the right, don't take the turning on the left to the beach (traeth). After a while the road bends to the left and becomes a dirt track. Follow this rough track as it heads

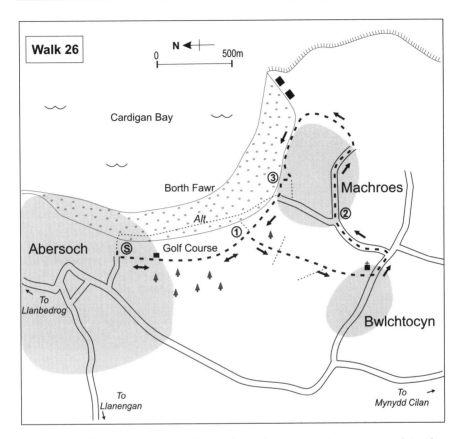

downhill to a coastal path. Follow this coastal path round to the left with the sea directly below you on the right.

There are fantastic views across the bay, Borth Fawr, to Abersoch and along the coast. In the distance you will be able to see the headland of Mynydd Tir-y-Cwmwd.

3. After you pass a boat yard to your right turn down a stony path which takes you to the beach.

There are benches on the sea front and toilets in the car park. Behind the toilets is a raised, grassy picnic area.

There are now two choices to return to the car. It is possible to walk all the way back to the car park along the beach if the tide is out, however this involves negotiating the wooden groynes.

Penrhyn Du from Machroes beach

The other option is to return through the golf course. To do this, turn left onto the path alongside the beach and follow this straight ahead into the golf course. Simply follow this track right the way through the golf course and back to your car.

In the area

Abersoch Maize Maze is an activity park with plenty to occupy the family. The maize maze has a certain theme each year. In the activity park there are trampolines, a kiddies' hay bale maze, go-karts and treasure hunts in the sand pit, or you can take a nature walk along the coastline (www.abersochmaze.co.uk).

Lleyn Hovercrafts, Tanrallt, Llangian, Abersoch – Great fun for all the family and a new experience in outdoor pursuits – hovercraft flying! Take a ride on a hovercraft, either as a passenger or take tuition to drive it yourself. Under 13's are only allowed as passengers with an instructor. Hovercrafts are single, two and four-seater. Booking essential (www.tanrallt.com).

Walk 27: Mynytho Common, Llanbedrog

Allow: 1 hour 30 minutes

Mynytho is a quiet village just outside Llanbedrog and has one of the most famous memorial halls in Wales, with a plaque bearing a poem by R Williams Parry, the renowned Welsh poet:

> *Adeiladwyd gan diodi – nid cerrig*
> *Ond cariad yw'r meini;*
> *Cydernes yw'r coed arni,*
> *Cyd-ddyheu a'l cododd hi.*

> *Built with poverty – not stones*
> *But love made the masonry;*
> *Its subscription is the woodwork,*
> *Joint aspiration got it built.*

The common to the north of the village is the location for this quiet walk, with lovely views south to Abersoch and St Tudwal's Islands (Ynysoedd Tudwal), and Mynydd Rhiw to the west. There is a picnic spot and view point in the car park, with toilets, and a children's playground can be found opposite the school.

Map: Ordnance Survey 1:25000 Explorer 253 – grid reference 302310

Distance: 2¼ miles (3.6 km)

Getting there: Drive along the B4413 from Llanbedrog to Botwnnog and take the small turning on your right at Mynytho. There is a small car park just off the road junction with toilets (closed out of season) and picnic tables. There is also a school and children's playground here.

Turn left out of the park and walk up past the school.

There are fantastic views down over the coast with Abersoch and St Tudwal's Islands to your right when you leave the car park.

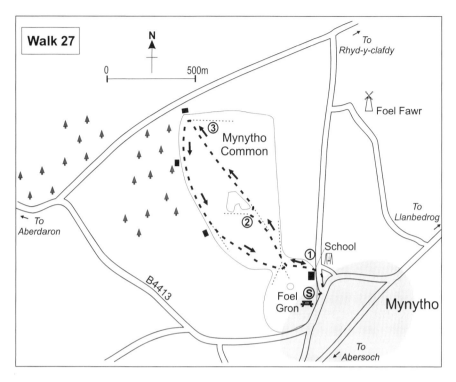

1. Take the footpath on the left immediately after the school (opposite the children's playground) signposted to Foel Gron. Follow
this track up as it curves to the right then continue straight ahead,
don't take the fork to the right.

The hill straight ahead is Mynydd Rhiw (Walk 25) and soon to your
right you will be able to see a small hill, Foel Fawr, with an old
windmill on the top. Hell's Mouth (Porth Neigwl) is now down on your
left.

Turn right at the fork in the path and then take the path that goes
diagonally across the common. This track bears left away from
the stone wall on your right. Then at the next fork in the path bear
left along the larger track.

If you take a minute to stop and look behind you will be able to see
the Harlech coast across the sea and the Rhinog mountains in the
Snowdonia National Park. Ahead of you is the hill Carn Fadryn.

Foel Fawr windmill

2. Turn right at the next junction with a walled enclosure ahead so that the wall is to your left. Then turn left at the crossroads at the next corner of the walled enclosure. Continue along with the wall on your left and at the far corner of the enclosure follow the path straight ahead, don't continue to go round the enclosure.

3. Turn left at the next junction from where you will be able to see a couple of houses and then left again at the next junction so you are heading back across the common away from the houses.

Walk along with the woodland on your right and when you pass a house the track narrows and runs alongside a stone wall. Once you pass a second cottage the track broadens and there are great coastal views to your right.

The track then curves round to the left and passes to the left of a small steep hill, Foel Gron. There are a couple of paths up this hill but if you want to go to the top we recommend you leave the pushchair at the bottom and take a papoose instead.

Bear right at the next junction, which brings you back to the track on which you started the walk. This track takes you back down to the road where you turn right and walk back to the car park.

In the area

Shearwater Coastal Cruises offer boat trips from Pwllheli Marina around St Tudwal's Islands and Hell's Mouth in the morning and evening. The afternoon trip also cruises round Bardsey Island. Trips are dependent on weather condition (www.shearwater.info).

Castellmarch Quad Bikes, Llanbedrog (07968 052079) has a safe, carefully marked track suitable for children of 6-11 years. A separate track is available for those over 12. The rides are led by marshals and treks can be 10 minutes or half an hour. Open in summer, Wednesday – Sunday from 1pm-5pm.

Walk 28: Carnguwch Church, Llwyndyrys

Allow: 45 minutes

This is a short, easy walk to an isolated church in the middle of nowhere! The church is on a hill by a stream, which would make a nice spot for a picnic. The bridge is also ideal for pooh-sticks!

The route is up a lane and permissive path through a farm, so take extra care to stick to the path. The track is fairly easy going, but there is a short steep climb to reach the church. It can be muddy in wet weather so wear boots or wellies.

Map: Ordnance Survey 1:25000 Explorer OL254 – grid reference 374410

Distance: 1½ miles (2 km)

Getting there: From the A499 take the minor road signposted to Llwyndyrys. Drive through the village and park on the verge on the far side, taking care not to block the road or any gateways.

Walk back into the village to the phone box and turn left up the lane. Go over the bridge and past the farm "Tyddyn Felin". Continue up the lane past a second house.

> Straight ahead of you is the smooth, rounded hill of Mynydd Carnguwch, with its large hilltop cairn. This pile of stones, actually a large Bronze Age burial mound, is said to have been thrown down by a giantess, who had carried them up there in her apron.

Carry on up the lane, ignoring a permissive track to the right, until you come to a farmyard.

1. Go into the farmyard and turn right keeping the house on your left to follow a permissive path.

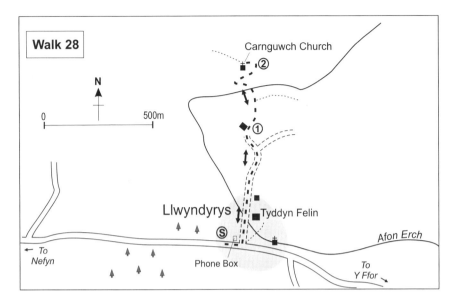

This is a working farm so stick to the path. Watch out for the enthusiastic dogs!

Go through a metal gate into a field and turn left to follow the wall.

Follow the grassy track as it zigzags down to a pretty little stream. Cross the bridge, taking care to close the gate and leave behind any dogs who may have followed you.

2. Once over the bridge, go up the grassy track to the church. The church is locked, but you can wander round the churchyard.

   This is the parish church of Carnguwch and dates from around 1721. It is dedicated to St Beuno, an early Celtic saint who is widely commemorated in North Wales. The church was rebuilt in 1828, and was undergoing further renovation at time of writing.

Retrace your steps back through the farmyard to the village and your car.

As you go down the hill, you can see the coast and St Tudwal's Islands off Pwllheli.

Path to Carnguwch church

In the area

Glasfryn Park near Pwllheli is an adventure park with go-karts, quad bikes, archery, bowling and fishing. Go-karting from 3 years old, quad biking from 6 years. Farm shop, café and children's play area on site. Open all year (www.glasfryn.co.uk).

Plas Talhenbont Hall Magical Grounds near Criccieth offers woodland walks in the Fool's Forest, birds in the Quackery and "Fort Good", the adventure playground. All animals can be fed and petted. Light refreshments available. Woodland walks may not be pushchair friendly but run along a beautiful riverside with plenty of picnic and paddling spots, so take the papoose. (01766 810247)

Walk 29: Lon Goed

Allow: 2 hours

Lon Goed is a unique tree-lined avenue running for a total of nearly 6 miles to the Lleyn coast at Afon Wen. It was built in the late 1700s to mid 1800s by the steward of the large local land owner at nearby Broom Hall to provide a route across the estate. He planted the avenue with hardwood trees, mainly oak and beech, which today provide an enchanting arched canopy.

To do the whole walk needs two cars, one at the start and one left at Afon Wen. As two cars need at least two people, we've stretched our three-stile rule for this walk, which includes five stiles/kissing gates, but we think it's worth the lifting to do the whole walk. If you are solo or only have one car, then it is possible to turn around about half way, at number 2, which is before the first stile.

Map: Ordnance Survey 1:25000 Explorer OL254 – grid reference 459433

Distance: 4 miles (7 km)

Getting there: From the A87 take the B4411 towards Criccieth. Take the first turning on the right, signposted Ynys Llangybi. Go past a farm on a sharp left-hand bend and follow the road ignoring the first left turn. Take the second left, marked with a blue bike sign and a small sign to "Ynys Galed", and follow it past felled trees and round a sharp left-hand bend where you will see the avenue of trees lining Lon Goed ahead of you. Park on the grass verge by a wooden notice board. To do the whole walk, leave a second car at Afon Wen on the A497 west of Criccieth (grid reference 439375). If there is no space here, then you can park in Chwilog on the B4354 (number 4).

Walk down the track through the trees, a mixture of oak and beech. Continue through two gates.

To your left is a lovely view across to the Nantlle Ridge and Moel Hebog, and behind you can see Snowdon.

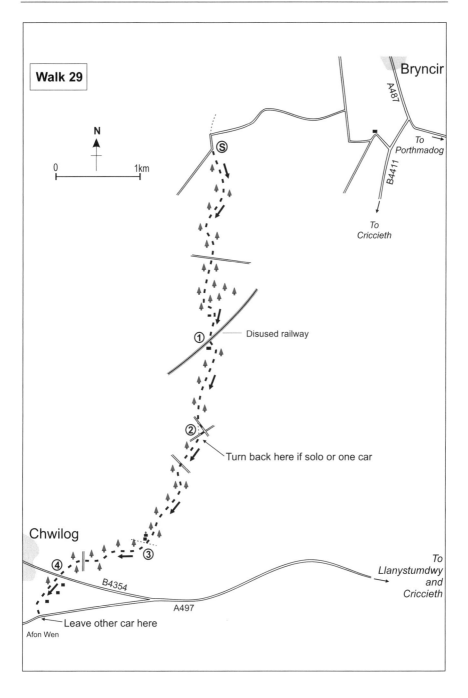

Walk 29

N

0   1km

Bryncir

A487

To
Porthmadog

B4411

To
Criccieth

S

Disused railway

① Turn back here if solo or one car

②

Chwilog

④   B4354   ③

To
Llanystumdwy
and
Criccieth

A497

Leave other car here

Afon Wen

Continue down the track, muddy in places, until you reach a lane. Cross the lane and continue down the track opposite, marked with a "Lon Goed" signpost.

1. Further down the track you come to a disused railway, with the original level crossing gate still in place and the house on your right was originally a railway building.

   This was the Caernarfon to Afon Wen line which opened in the 1860s. This railway was a continuation of the start of the line now operated by the Welsh Highland Railway in Caernarfon (Walk 19). A ballad was written about an accident on this line at Bryncir, which killed six members of a Calvinistic society returning from a meeting in Caernarfon. The line closed in 1964.

   Continue down the track until you reach an angular T-junction. Ignore the signposted kissing gate opposite and instead, turn left and walk down the road to a cross-roads.

2. At the cross-roads, turn right, pass a ladder stile on the right and turn left through a wooden gate (signposted) to re-join Lon Goed. This gate is partially blocked and you may need to lift the push-chair over the gate.

   If you are solo or only have one car, turn back here to walk back the way you came.

   Continue down the track, through a gate to cross a road, and through another gate next to a kissing gate (too narrow for the pushchair). Carry on to a fence with a kissing gate, which you need to lift over.

   Here, you join a farm track, which turns to the left. Continue along the track until a right-hand bend, where you take the left fork through woodland, not up towards the house.

   Go over a cattle grid or through the adjacent gate, and continue along the track.

3. When you come to a chapel, continue straight ahead and through

a metal gate. Continue
until you get to a stone
wall with a kissing
gate. Lift over the gate
and look out for your
first view of the sea in
the distance!

After the gate, the
track becomes grassy.
Go through a gate, past
some slate slabs and
across another lane.

4. When you come to a
main road, cross it
with care and
continue down Lon
Goed directly oppo-
site.

Lon Goed

The village of Chwilog is
500m to the right and
is an option for leaving your other car.

Pass a house on your left and when the track bends round to the
right take the left fork to continue straight ahead along the line of
trees, where the path becomes narrower.

Lift over a kissing gate and continue along a grassy path. Zigzag
around the walls and lift over a green wooden kissing gate. Ahead
there are nice views of the coast.

Look closely and you'll see that many of the walls round here are
actually earth banks faced with stone. These are traditional
cloddiau (clawdd is the single) and are similar in construction to
Devon banks and Cornish hedges. Many have organised stone
facing, usually with vertically arranged stones, but you may also
see herringbone patterns or, if large boulders are incorporated, a

random arrangement at the base. Cloddiau tend to be vegetated – the tops are capped by turf or hedges and the stonework may be obscured by grass.

Go through a metal gate next to a kissing gate and continue down to the main road at Afon Wen where you left your other car.

In the area

Dwyfor Ranch Rabbit Farm (01766 523136) has various breeds of rabbits and friendly farm animals including ponies, lambs and kids. This is a good rainy day activity as a large number of the rabbits are in farm buildings. Children are allowed to handle baby rabbits and sheepdog puppies and feed farmyard animals under supervision. Take a ride on the free pony-and-trap. Light refreshments are available. Open daily Easter to end of October, 10am – 6pm

Criccieth Castle is located on a dramatic headland with spectacular views over Snowdonia. Originally a Welsh castle, built by Llywelyn the Great around 1240 it was later captured by the English and re-fortified. The castle was eventually captured and burnt by Owain Glyndwr and the scorch marks and still visible today. An excellent place for little imaginations to run wild! Open April – October.

Walk 30: Y Cob, Porthmadog

Allow: 1 hour 30 minutes (not including train journey)

Porthmadog is situated at the very north-eastern point of the Lleyn Peninsula where it joins the main mass of Wales. Built on the estuary of the Glaslyn and Dwyryd Rivers, the town is rich in maritime history. It is named after William A. Maddocks who helped with the development of the town as a major slate port for the quarries of Blaenau Ffestiniog.

Today, the town is also a railway hub with stations for the mainline from Mid-Wales to Pwllheli, the Ffestiniog Railway and the southern end of the Welsh Highland Railway. This walk starts with a trip on the Ffestiniog Railway before bringing you back to town via woodlands around Portmeirion and the Cob built across the estuary. You can either just travel to the first station, or do the walk to complete a day out on the railway.

Map: Ordnance Survey 1:25000 Explorer OL18 – Grid reference 571384

Distance: 3 miles (5 km)

Getting there: Park in the Ffestiniog Railway car park in Porthmadog. There is a café, pub, shop and toilets at the station.

Take the steam train from Porthmadog to the first station at Minffordd.

The guards are very helpful and they will put the pushchair in the guard's van if you ask. It is also worth telling them where you are alighting so that they are ready to help with the pushchair at the station. This is a relatively short train journey but it takes you across the Cob with fantastic coastal views to your right and views up the Glaslyn estuary to your left.

1. Leave the train at the first stop, Minffordd Station. Turn right and walk to the end of the station where you will find an exit onto the

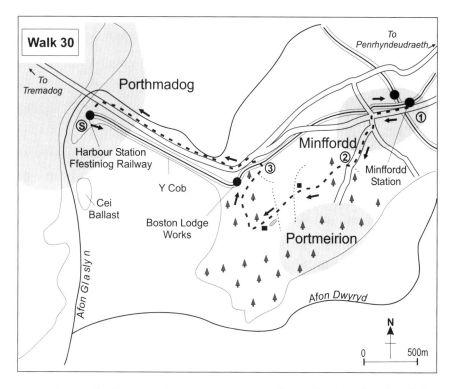

main road. Stay on the pavement on the right-hand side of the road walking back in the direction of Porthmadog (this involves a quick step onto the road to pass round a wall so watch out for traffic). When you come to a bus shelter cross the road at the pedestrian crossing and turn immediately left up towards Portmeirion Village and Gardens.

Take the first turning on the right in the direction of Portmeirion. Then just after this turning move onto the footpath on the left, which runs alongside this road.

There are lovely views over Tremadog and surrounding hills to your right. Soon you will also be able to see the Dwyryd estuary down on your left and the small island of Ynys Gifftan.

2. When you come to a crossroads turn right up the bridlepath. This path is rocky to begin with but soon evens out.

If you want to visit Portmeirion (see "In the Area") first then continue along the footpath ahead and simply return to this point once you are done. There are toilets in the Portmeirion car park.

When you come to a junction go up through the gateway straight ahead and into a field. Follow the wall to your right across the field and this brings you to a farm. Go through the old gateposts and down the path to a crossroads. Continue straight ahead here on the broad track, which takes you up to a cattle grid with adjoining gate. Go straight ahead again here towards a second farm passing a pond on your left.

Continue straight ahead at the farm, not left up to the farm itself. The path can be quite muddy here. This takes you across another field and up to a small gate (there is a second gate to your left). Do not go through the gate but turn right and follow the fence along the field.

There are fantastic views down the coast of the Lleyn Peninsular from here. The Glaslyn estuary is directly below you with the Cob down to your right. The headland just on the other side of the estuary is Ynys Cyngar.

Follow the path as it curves to the left to a gateway, which takes you into the woodland. This path then goes round to the right following the course of the headland with the Cob directly below you.

3. The path takes you down through the woodland and, just after a path joins in from the right, you will come down to the railway line. Go through the large gates and cross over the railway line watching out for steam trains. Follow the path down to the road.

Cross over the road (look for the round tollhouse to the Cob), turn left and walk along the pavement. The pavement takes you under an archway, past some information boards and onto the cycle path. There is a bird hide to the right here. Follow the cycle path across the Cob.

The Cob was built between 1808 and 1811 by William Maddocks in

Porthmadog Harbour Station with trainspotters!

order to reclaim marshy land from the sea. This was all part of a
scheme to make Porthmadog, Tremadog and the Cob with its
tollhouse an integral part of the journey to Ireland, which would
have been from Porth Dinllaen. Unfortunately for him, in 1810 the
decision was made to use Holyhead as the main Irish Port and
Maddocks nearly went bust with all the expenditure. He was saved
by the growth of the slate industry, and Porthmadog became the
major port for slate shipped around the world from Blaenau
Ffestiniog.

There are several benches along this stretch of path from which to
admire the lovely views up the Glaslyn estuary.

At the end of the cycle path go straight ahead and walk along the
pavement. Cross the road and find your car in the station car
park.

In the area

Portmeirion is an Italianate village created between 1926 and 1976 by the architect Clough Williams-Ellis on his own private peninsula (www.portmeirion-village.com). It is the origin of Portmeirion pottery and was the setting for the TV series "The Prisoner". You can have an intriguing day out wandering round the buildings and browsing in the small shops. You can also walk through pretty subtropical gardens and woodland (easy paths) on the shore of the estuary and walk on the extensive sandy beach (tide times are shown on all entry tickets). Most of the village is accessible by pushchair, though there are some steps. There is a café and toilets with baby changing facilities. Dogs are not allowed in the village.

The Ffestiniog Railway (www.festrail.co.uk) is a narrow-gauge steam railway running along the Vale of Ffestiniog from Porthmadog to Blaenau Ffestiniog. It is the oldest independent railway company in the world and runs steam trains throughout the summer months and a combination of diesel and steam the rest of the year. There are special children's events throughout the year and a "Talking Train" runs daily at noon, giving you stories and information about the area. Porthmadog and Tan-y-Bwlch Stations have cafés with highchairs and baby changing facilities.

More Pushchair Walks from Sigma:

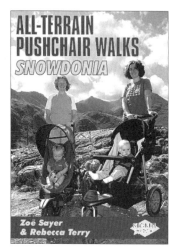
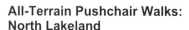
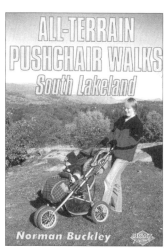